Ruby Shoes

by Michele Zumwalt

*A true story about a devastating
prescription addiction tornado,
being lost in a strange world
and the precious gift
that brought me
HOME.*

Book cover design by Judy Bullard, www.customebookcovers.com

This book is not intended as a substitute for the medical advice of physicians. The reader should regularly consult a physician in matters relating to his/her health and particularly with respect to any symptoms that may require diagnosis or medical attention.

THE HOLY BIBLE, NEW INTERNATIONAL VERSION®, NIV® Copyright © 1973, 1978, 1984, 2011 by Biblica, Inc.™ Used by permission. All rights reserved worldwide.

The Twelve Steps are reprinted with the permission of Alcoholics Anonymous World Services, Inc. Permission to reprint and adapt the Twelve Steps does not mean that AA has reviewed or approved the contents of this publication, nor that AA agrees with the views expressed herein. AA is a program of recovery from alcohol only – use of the Twelve Steps in connection with programs and activities which are patterned after AA, but which address other problems, does not imply otherwise.

Printed in the United States of America, First Printing, 2015

ISBN-13: 978-1512080865

ISBN-10: 1512080861

Three Wire Publishing, P.O. Box 2094, Folsom, California 95763, 3wirepublishing.com

Author Contact information:

Michele Zumwalt

Email: michele@zumwaltinc.com

Or on Facebook: Michele Zumwalt

Praise for Ruby Shoes

"Michele Zumwalt has written a powerful book about prescription drug addiction. She speaks from the heart and from experience, having overcome her own addiction to painkillers. This book will strike a chord with anyone struggling with addiction."

Rod Colvin, Author

Overcoming Prescription Drug Addiction

"In nearly two decades of medical practice as an internal medicine physician, I have seen that it is only God in Christ who heals those suffering from the bondage of addiction, and that He uses special instruments to accomplish His amazing purposes. Michele Zumwalt is one such instrument, and her book most certainly has been divinely inspired. Her heartfelt story will touch all whose lives have been impacted by the devastation of addiction, and shows the glory of The Lord to make all things new in a powerful story of redemption."

Ingvild Gangsaas Lane, MD

"Michele Zumwalt was brave beyond compare to share her journey through addiction. She has written in juxtaposition of the tale of Dorothy in Oz with her own tale of finding her way back. The book weaves spirituality, current statistics of addiction, 12-step recovery and her wit and wisdom of her truth to bring us to the reality of finding hope for those who are lost and cannot find their way back home. I loved it!"

Susan Kelleher, California Department of Justice,

Wellness Coordinator, Retired

DEDICATION

To those who are lost,

you are loved by God who knows right where you are.

To my mother, Donna Perry, who loved me completely,

as God did, even in my most broken place. She never gave

up on me, but kept pointing to our only hope.

Jesus.

Foreword

This book is a story of hope. It is written to reach the prescription addict and alcoholic. However, it is also intended to reach those who have witnessed and been involved in their struggles: parents, spouses, relatives, friends, churches and recovery groups. It is a story of one woman's journey from total prescription addiction to her return to God.

Her father and I lived this entire journey with her. We flew back and forth from southern California to northern California to be with her when she was hospitalized. I was with her when she was going through her handbag for more medications *while in the hospital*. When I took her handbag away, she became angry and screamed, "I don't need you here! You go home and leave me alone! I hate you!" I knew that this was the addict talking and not the daughter we raised. There was a nurse's station just outside her room in ICU and I asked the nurse to get a doctor for me immediately. The nurse asked me who I was and I told her that I was her mother. She began to tell me that my daughter was a "legal" adult and that I had no rights to have any input. I said loudly, "If you do not get a doctor here immediately, I am going to start screaming!" When a young doctor rushed in, I told him about the handbag issue and that my daughter was a prescription addict. He said that they had considered the possibility. He stopped a planned transfer to another hospital for further testing. He said, "These tests would likely have killed her".

Her father and I were exasperated and our feelings were raw. Still, we did not give up on her. We prayed, as did our family, church and many prayer warriors. Her father told her that she was more important than anything. He added that he was prepared to "give up his job" and follow her every move. Money was really unimportant at this point in our lives.

Several years later, we were with her in ICU in another hospital. A doctor told me that she might not make it this time. She was jerking all over and was not responsive. When she calmed down somewhat, I left just long enough to pray in the hospital chapel. I pleaded to God to save her life. It was during this hospital stay in ICU, in her state of semi consciousness, that she also began to plea for her life and fully surrendered to God. You see, we all loved her! But, she, alone, was the only one who had the power to give up her years of struggle to her God.

Her first try at sobriety was in the Care Unit in Orange, California. It was there that I gave her a magnet with a quote from the Bible, Jeremiah 29:11, "For I know the plans I have for you says the Lord...to give you a future and a hope". She kept this throughout her years of addiction and it has remained on her refrigerator. She mentioned to me many times that she read this daily for so many years. Still, she refers to it.

Today, our daughter, Michele Zumwalt, is a shining example for all who come in contact with her. She is involved in church leadership, serves as a police chaplain, is an active participant in 12 Step Recovery Programs, is executive director of a charity benefiting children (Contractors Caring for Kids) and speaks at various group meetings to share her story.

My final comment to all who read this is NEVER GIVE UP! GOD IS STILL IN CHARGE AND HE STILL WORKS MIRACLES!

Dr. Donna W. Perry

ACKNOWLEDGMENTS

One thing's sure, this book would not have been written were it not for the tremendous assistance I've received from my mom, Dr. Donna Perry. She has been the chief editor of this book and, in every way possible; she is the editor of my life. I love you, Mom. Thank you also to my dad, James Perry, who has helped a great deal with reading, editing, and critiquing this book. My husband, John and my daughters, Sarah and Katie, who continue to encourage me to write and serve those who still suffer. I will spend my *whole* life thanking God for the gift of you. My father, Joe Penn and Sandy Penn and all of my Texas family, I thank you for the love and encouragement. Thank you for the continual review of biblical references used in this book and helping to ensure sound teaching. My brothers, Scott, Deck, Jim and Pat, and my little sister, Elizabeth, your prayers and words of encouragement have always sustained me. My friend, Robin Drummond, is mentioned in the book and is someone who I can always count on for the love and encouragement I need to keep going, no matter what. Thank you Dr. Ingvild Lane and Susan Kelleher for the help in editing and for your valued friendship. My recovery, church, and chaplain friends are too many to mention, but the difference you've made in my life could never be expressed in the written word. All of the people in my life have pointed me to one place for my source of strength. Thank you, Jesus, for loving me and saving me, even from myself.

Ruby Shoes

Table of Contents

Part One: Prescription Addiction

Part Two: Recovery – My Way

Part Three: Recovery - God's Way

Part One: Prescription Addiction

Michele Zumwalt

Chapter One

Lost

It was a beautiful, sunny morning in California on July 20, 2009. As I left the house for my usual early morning run, I felt energized and optimistic about the day ahead. Some time ago, I'd developed the habit of talking to God while running, mostly because I needed His help to get my exercise routine completed. This morning was like all the others. I thanked God for all that He was doing in my life and asked for His guidance and protection.

For some time, I had been talking to God about a desire of my heart to write a very personal story. You see, I almost died from an addiction to prescription drugs, but He saved me from certain death. Since coming into recovery many years ago, I have seen countless people die from this devastating problem. I've seen lives destroyed and families ripped apart. So, I was praying that day about writing this story of *hope* for the millions of people still trapped in the hopeless prescription addiction pit that I had escaped.

Long ago, my grandparents had given me a plaque with the scripture from Psalm 37:4 *"Delight yourself in the LORD; And He will give you the desires of your heart."* I keep that plaque in my bedroom because it reminds me to seek God's will *first* in my life and then the desire of my heart will always be to do His will. That July morning, I was asking God all the same questions about His will for me. Should I write this book? Was this the right time? Are You *sure* You want *me* to do this? As I topped the hill by my home, I came upon a piece of paper on the ground. I stepped over it and kept on running. After all, it was only a piece of trash. For some reason, I turned around and picked it up. On that piece of paper was God's answer to my prayer. Written on the paper was this:

TELL YOUR STORY

Read: Mark 5:1-20

"Go home to your friends, and tell them what great things the Lord has done for you, and how He has had compassion on you." *Mark 5:19*. It was a story of a possessed man who was set free by Jesus from the demons that had controlled him his entire life. The man was so happy to finally be free that all he wanted to do was follow Jesus around. He wanted to stay close to his Savior and worship Him. Jesus told him to go home and tell his personal story to others. He reminded the

man that by telling his story, he would help them. I could really relate to the message Jesus gave him.

I was so excited! With tears in my eyes, I think I read and re-read that little typewritten page about ten times on my way home. I had asked God a question that morning and in a *very direct way*, He had answered my question.

And so, I began writing my story. I have to confess that over the last few years, my desire to tell this story perfectly has slowed me down some. I've come to realize that I cannot write, or do anything for that matter, perfectly. Only God is perfect. More specifically, His love for us is perfect. *1 John 4:12 says, "If we love one another, God abides in us and His love is perfected in us."* It was God's perfect, saving love in my most sinful moments of complete brokenness and utter despair that made all the difference for me. His perfect love has led me to feel a deep and abiding love for so many others who are still lost in horrors of prescription addiction. So, it is for them that I tell my story.

Several years ago, my daughter played a small role in a community theater group's performance of "The Wizard of Oz." I was overwhelmed by the realization that this, in so many ways, was a metaphor for the story of my life. Like Dorothy, I was a restless young person. Although I had a good life, I felt insecure, vulnerable, and afraid. I knew the impending doom of Dorothy in the first black and white scenes of the movie. I found myself caught up in a violent storm that forever changed my life. I was hopelessly lost in a deadly prescription addiction tornado that ripped my life apart and carried me so far away from home that I was sure I'd never survive. I almost didn't.

Lost in a strange world, I searched, as she did, to find answers to my questions and all the while, I just wanted to go home. I followed good advice, did what I was told to do, and still I couldn't escape this odd and foreign place. I tried everything to get back home, even chasing brooms when a wizard promised the captured broom would save me. I changed the law in California and even took that captured broom on national television. On the CBS Evening News, "Eye on America," I told the world about the problem of prescription addiction and how I intended to work to solve it and save others in the future. I believed that if I captured enough of the world's brooms, that I could make it back home.

After years of struggle in countless vain attempts to please an impossible wizard, I discovered the truth. Oz, or the world, was full of ordinary people with no extraordinary power at all. No matter what I achieved for this world, it would never save me. I would never be able to get back home.

It was only from that utterly defeated place that I could finally surrender in acceptance of a precious and powerful gift that I had been given long ago. This is my discovery journey of survival and my final surrender to Jesus. It is a true story of His redemptive love and of hope for the future.

To tell you a little about myself today, I live a simple, but full life of hope and recovery in Folsom, California. I love big hair, Aqua Net hairspray, running, good books, Bible studies with the church ladies, homemade lemon meringue pie from our lemon tree, and Sunday dinners with the *whole* family. I am a happily married wife and mother of two beautiful daughters. I also have two golden retrievers, or my furry kids. While my furry kids quietly demonstrate the golden rule for our family members with skin, my husband and daughters vibrantly demonstrate God's love and compassion for our whole world. Our oldest daughter, Sarah, just returned from Africa where she served as a missionary. With grateful hearts, "love and service to God and others" is our family mission. Through this devastating addiction, my faith in God has grown exponentially and I know, today, that I am surrounded by the best friends and family on the planet.

My college degree is in Business Marketing and I've worked with my husband as a small business employer for more the 25 years. I also serve as a Law Enforcement Chaplain for Sacramento County. Before that I worked as a Marketing Executive with Xerox Corporation. So, how *did* I end up with an addiction that almost killed me? How did I fall so far, so fast? I went from a good kid, happy home, with a successful career to a completely hopeless prescription drug addict having a seizure, a stoke and even going to jail.

Since the addiction which almost took my life, I've asked those questions many times. While I don't have all the answers, I have become a person who is passionate about the problem of prescription addiction and helping others survive it. I know if *I* can get better, *anyone* can. Sometimes, these days, I'm so overwhelmed with joy and gratitude for the life I have, I feel I could burst. I know I have to give it away to keep it. Therefore, I am an advocate for recovery, a public speaker, an active church and community volunteer, a Law Enforcement Chaplain, and a teacher of 12-Step recovery and biblical life applications.

Like Dorothy, I grew up in a Christian home, in a southern state, and was always surrounded with a great deal of love and support. My mom and dad met at the Texas state FFA (Future Farmers of America) and the FHA (Future Homemakers of America) conventions. My dad was the Texas State FFA President and my mom was the Texas State FHA President. They were young, talented, and beautiful. When they were married, it seemed like a storybook wedding, but it was never to have that happily ever after ending part. They were just too young to marry and sadly, for both families, they divorced when I was just a toddler. A divorce in the 1960's, and in the Bible belt no less, was perhaps one of the worst things that could happen to two young people who had so much hope and promise for their lives. They would tell you that the one good thing that came out of it all was me and while the divorce was difficult for both families, I always felt loved and needed by everyone.

Eventually, my parents both remarried the most wonderful people and for more than four decades, I've been blessed with two families who've always loved me and wanted me close to them. My mom married her high school sweetheart from Lubbock, Texas. He was a Navy pilot and is one of the best people I've ever known. I have no memory of not living with James Perry. He is the dad who has been with me day in and day out for all of my life. They had two more children, my little sister, Elizabeth, and a younger brother, Scott, and in every sense of the word, we were and still are a family. We've always been a very close family and, like all close families, our struggles have bound us even tighter together. Likewise, my real dad met and married the most incredible stepmom ever. He married Sandy when I was seven. She was only twelve years older than me and I thought she was one of the most exciting and fun people I'd ever met. She probably hated it, but when I'd come to visit at Christmas and summer vacations, Sandy would play board games like Monopoly with me for hours on end. To this day and always, Sandy is a blessing in all of our lives. They had three boys, Deck, Jim, and Pat. They are all married with children and living in Texas. I keep in close contact with both sides of my family.

As a child I would travel back and forth between the two families. While I lived with my mom, I knew that my dad wanted me to live with him also. In my childish thinking, I began to feel that each family *needed* me with them. I felt responsible for their happiness and, even at a young age, I started to adapt to my environment. I would go to one home and say that I really wanted to be with them all the time. Then, I would go to the other home and say the same thing. The more I pretended the worse I felt. It was like a growing snowball of deceit.

It's a sad fact that in my 12-Step meetings today, I often hear people talk about having no one in their lives who really loves them or cares about them. Many feel that no one has ever really wanted them around. I've often felt guilty about the fact that I've spent so much time complaining about how difficult it was for me when everyone wanted me with them. Even still, the fact remains that some of my earliest feelings were of shame and guilt because I knew that I was being dishonest with both families. I sensed their insecurity and sadness and I learned to do everything I could to make them feel better. I'd quite literally transform myself on airplane rides depending on which direction the flight was headed. I was becoming a shell, an empty dwelling of my former self. All that mattered was pleasing the people around me. I thought if they were happy, I'd be happy.

Later in my life, a recovery counselor suggested that there are two kinds of happiness in this world, big "H" Happy and little "h" happy. Little "h" is the kind of happiness that comes from all the outside stuff like a great job, a fancy car, a big home, and everyone's good opinion of me. While little "h" happiness is good, it is nothing like the *joy* found in big "H" Happy. Big "H" Happiness comes from all the inside stuff. It comes from being the person God designed me to be. With Big "H" Happiness, my life has meaning and purpose. Only though seeking Big "H" am I able to live the life that God intended for me all along.

Over the years, I've come to understand that while they are both happiness, they do have some important differences. We cannot always control little "h" happiness. Sometimes, we do everything right and still lose that job, car, home, or even other people's approval of us. Perhaps, we invest our money wisely and still lose it. Other times, we are unfairly judged by others and people disappoint or betray us. Sometimes, there are just never enough people around to sing our praises and bring some much needed little "h" happiness for the day. Contrarily, we can *always* have big "H" Happiness. With God's help, we can always match calamity with serenity.

During those early years, I knew nothing about how important Big "H" Happiness was or even how to begin looking for it. I spent my teenage years and early adult life trying to make little "h" happiness into Big "H" Happiness. I had a competitive spirit and desire to be the best at everything I did. I was always on the hunt for more happiness. I figured, if you liked me enough or if I were successful enough, I'd be happy. In high school I was Student Body President, selected each year for Homecoming Court, Girl's State Senator, and so on. I started college in

1982 with a full academic scholarship to the University of Arkansas and transferred to finish at California State University, Sacramento. I loved school and was a very involved student.

My life was good, at least from the outside looking in. But on the inside, I felt driven to keep doing more, accomplishing more, getting more out of life. As long as I can remember, my outsides never matched my insides. I could put on a smile and go, but being authentic wasn't part of the plan. I began to feel as if my value as a person was contingent upon my accomplishments, which were never quite enough. *Little "h" was perhaps my first drug and I was hooked.* There was a hole inside me that seemed to be temporarily filled with each accomplishment or recognition. But, that hole would quickly empty and grow bigger. I was lost and alone and my fear was turning into desperation.

In the black and white portion of the movie, The Wizard of Oz, Dorothy was overwhelmed with fear that Toto would be "destroyed" by that evil Mrs. Gulch. I didn't have a real life Mrs. Gulch trying to destroy something that I loved. I just know, that for as long as I can remember, I was afraid. No one ever tried to make me fearful, but I lived with a constant sense of impending doom. Whether it was fear of losing something I had or not getting something I needed, fear was my constant companion.

There were some ominous warnings which might have served to alert me of the coming tornado. My first experience with alcohol in college was a good example of the darkening skies rolling into my life. As I mentioned, I started college at the University of Arkansas. I loved so many things about college life. The campus was beautiful, my classes were interesting, and there was always something fun going on. Lou Holtz was the head football coach when I was at the University of Arkansas and the pep rallies alone were thrilling, not to mention the games. The exciting world of sororities and fraternities on campus, with all their cool parties and activities, was a new experience for this small town girl. I was ready for it all, or so I thought.

One day, early in my freshman year, I was getting ready for the big Arkansas Razorbacks football game. I was trying to make it a perfect day for everyone and was exhausted from all the planning. I had found the right date, the perfect outfit to wear, right parties to attend, friends to go with and on and on it went. Hours later, with my big 80's hair all done up, I was finally ready.

When we arrived at one of the pre-game fraternity parties, they had this huge bowl of punch filled with what tasted like Kool-Aid. I quickly learned that special party punch had an important ingredient called, Everclear, (which is pure grain alcohol). That Everclear punch was delicious! After a couple of drinks, I remember actually thinking, "Wow, this is so much easier than what I have been doing." It was so simple to just take a drink and suddenly feel fine with the world around me. Drinking that Everclear Kool-

Aid, I found that I was at peace and it took no effort at all. I didn't care if he liked me, if you liked me, if we won the game, if my makeup was still perfect or even if my hair was still big. Life was suddenly easy and the world was just as it should be.

There is a promise in the "The Big Book of Alcoholic's Anonymous" which perfectly describes my feelings that day. That promise comes after the 9th step and it is, "We will comprehend the word *serenity* and we will know peace." After a couple of drinks from that spiked college punch, I could comprehend the word serenity and I *knew peace.* In fact, it was a peace like I had never known before. So, I began my search for serenity, the easier softer way. This was so much better than what I'd been doing by chasing after that ever fleeting little "h" happiness. You never could count on little "h" anyway. This college punch could be counted on anytime, day or night. I later came to realize that those 12-Steppers were talking about another way of life. The serenity and peace they were referring to involved living a life fully relying on God.

Long ago, they used to call alcohol, "Spirits" and I was searching for a spirit. Of course, I didn't know at the time that I was really searching for God. The problem was that the spirits found in a college punch bowl could never be the One True Spirit that I so desperately needed. Years later, someone in a recovery meeting said that he had a huge God-sized hole in him and his description of that God-sized hole fit me perfectly. He talked about spending years of his life trying to fill that hole with everything *except* God. He said that there was never enough of all the world offered to fill his God-sized hole.

During that semester, I realized that I was hanging out by the punch bowl a bit too often and I probably wasn't going to be a top student at the University of Arkansas. Being an immature kid, I figured that if I cannot be the best at something, then I don't want to do it at all. I began a pattern that my recovery friends today call, "a cut and run" or pulling a "geographic." So, rather than stepping away from the punch bowl, and digging into my studies, I just called my dad who had moved the family to Sacramento, California and I transferred out to finish college there.

You know how they say, wherever you go, there you are? In California, I immediately fell right back into my old people-pleasing, little "h" happy-seeking behavior. I once again focused all my attention on what my husband calls, "taking care of the look good." I got involved in church again with my family, not because I was seeking God's will in my life, but because that's what good kids do. They go to church. I stayed away from alcohol and I studied hard, not because I thought drinking was a problem, but because that's what good kids do. They don't drink and they make good grades. I helped with many church and community service projects mostly because that's what good girls do and, as an added bonus, it looks good on a resume.

My junior year I was selected as Camellia Princess from California State University, Sacramento. The Sacramento area has a Camellia festival which is like the Rose Parade in Pasadena, California, only on a much smaller scale. It was high school all over again. I really felt I was doing well because the world around me liked me, or at least the "me" they were seeing. Of course, they didn't know the *real* me. I didn't even know the *real* me. I never let myself think about what I wanted. I simply accomplished things in my life to help fill that ever-growing hole inside me. I seemed to be needing more and more attention and recognition from others as time went on.

After I graduated from college in May of 1986, I started a great job with Xerox Corporation. At Xerox, I was promoted quickly and at one point, I was the youngest person in the country working as a product specialist for a new computer system. I eagerly accepted this promotion. Failure never occurred to me; it was simply not an option. I genuinely felt that I would be happy if I was successful, but my life felt crazy and out of control. Even with all the recognition I received from Xerox, family, and friends, it was sustaining me less and less. Just like any other drug, I seemed to need more and more praise from everyone around me. There was never enough little "h" happiness to maintain my *high*. I was lost.

Then, the headaches began. I had had some in college, but nothing prepared me for what came at me in 1986 and

1987. My headaches were debilitating. I would get so sick that I would be in bed for days. Nothing had ever slowed me down like the pain I had during that time.

To help with the headaches, I started taking prescription medication. At first it was just the relief I needed. I didn't have to hurt anymore and I didn't have to think about how to be happy and keep getting the attention and recognition that I seemed to always need from everyone around me. It felt just like being back at the punch bowl at the University of Arkansas. Prescriptions were easy. I could just float away.

I needed to escape because I was so lost. I wasn't happy and I hadn't been for a while. I felt empty and tired. Nothing in my life was Big "H" Happy. Always running and chasing after that stupid little "h" and I could never count on it. I wish I could tell you that I reached out to God, to my church, to my family, but I did not. I sank into the abyss of prescription drugs and into the devil's hands. As the clouds grew darker with each passing day, the winds of the tornado began to whirl around me and I was blindly swept away by narcotic prescription medications.

Michele Zumwalt

Chapter Two

Tornado

Addiction to prescription medications hit me as fast and with as much fury as that tornado in Kansas hit Dorothy and Toto. It was sudden and it was devastating. How did this happen to me? How did I end up here? Was I born with a genetic predisposition towards addiction or did I cross a line somehow? Alcohol and prescription medications had never been a major part of my life. Still, here I was in a relatively short amount of time.

The addiction started like this. One day I had a headache and the blue sky started getting darker and the next day, I was whirling around in the center of the huge twister. I was completely powerless to escape its wrath and I had no way of controlling where, or if, I'd ever come out of it alive. I was being whirled around by a force much more powerful than me.

When I first saw a doctor for help with my headaches, I was almost immediately given shot cards for administering Demerol, a powerful opiate narcotic medication. My Health Maintenance Organization (HMO) at the time had a policy which allowed a patient to get what they called, "shot cards" for a certain number of injections without having to see a doctor every time. It was a way of saving money for the HMO, but for me, shot cards were the vehicle which drove me right into the epicenter of the tornado.

I was probably addicted to Demerol even before I knew what it was called. I would simply go into the injection stations, present my card and receive my shot. Demerol was such a powerful narcotic that it was only a short time before I needed a shot almost every day. Soon, I needed them *every* day. Then, I needed them *several times* throughout the day. My headaches seemed to be worsening. I would need another shot as soon as the pain medication wore off. I didn't know at the time that I was actually suffering from rebound headaches caused by narcotics. My solution was quickly becoming my problem. The monster storm grew in strength and spun me around faster and faster.

The use of shot cards and the absence of medical supervision might have facilitated the ease and suddenness with which I became a severely drug dependent person, but how I became addicted certainly didn't matter much given my condition. Looking back, two things are clear to me today. First, shot cards were a bad idea. Demerol is a scheduled narcotic, which means that the use of these medications requires a great deal of medical supervision, tracking, and record keeping. Scheduled narcotics are tracked very closely by state and federal government agencies, including the Drug Enforcement Agency because they are highly addictive and can be dangerous drugs. In my case, this wasn't happening. Second, I was probably addicted to Demerol even before I knew much about it. Demerol is an opiate like morphine or heroin. With prolonged use of opiates, like Demerol, the question isn't *if* the person will become addicted, but *when* they will become addicted. After the addiction took over, the doctors could not help me out of the ferocious and deadly tornado. In fact, they often unknowingly and maybe even well intentioned, made my situation worse.

How does a person become addicted to prescriptions? There are two camps of thought from the medical community regarding the problem of prescription addiction. The first camp says that these are highly addictive medications which require a great deal of care and attention when being prescribed. I once knew a doctor in this camp and he explained that everyone who takes opiates over long periods of time becomes addicted to them. The doctor referred to studies with laboratory animals. Each one of them became addicted to opiates over the course of time. He told me that these drugs were designed to be used *after surgery,* or *after a traumatic injury,* or in the case of a person *with a terminal illness* where addiction would not be a life changing problem. These drugs, he told me, were not appropriate for chronic pain problems like headaches.

There is another school of thinking in the medical community about the problem of prescription addiction. This second camp says that a person can *never* become addicted to narcotics *if* they are taking the medication for *real* pain and *if* it is taken as prescribed. From my personal experience, they are flat out wrong. I had real pain and was taking narcotics as prescribed and yet I ended up addicted. It's a convenient idea though, if you're a doctor or an HMO, because in this scenario, they would never have any responsibility for a patient becoming addicted to prescriptions. If this were actually true, then why in the world would we even bother to schedule and regulate these narcotics? Why would we pay so many agencies to oversee their use and why would we have so many people addicted to prescriptions in our country?

I spent many years in early recovery trying to understand the hows and the whys of prescription addiction, but it never changed the fact that I was in the fight of my life with this deadly storm raging within me. And once addicted, I went to places that I *never* thought I'd go. Over the next three years, I became another person altogether. My whole purpose for living was about getting pain medication and feeding my addiction.

When I would take narcotics, I'd often forget how much I had taken. A couple of times, I awoke in an ER with a doctor telling me that I would have certainly died had they not pumped out my stomach. I don't recall ever feeling suicidal, although I certainly struggled with depression during that period of my life. Then again, who wouldn't be depressed? Drugs and alcohol are depressants, so they contribute to making us feel down in the dumps. Almost everyone I've ever known coming into recovery is depressed.

The amount of grace I received during this very dangerous part of my life was probably more than I will ever fully comprehend. I am reminded of this scripture, *"But by the grace of God I am what I am, and His grace to me was not without effect...the grace of God that was with me."* 1 Corinthians 15:10

Having my stomach pumped out at the hospital was never something I thought would happen to me. Drinking and driving was not something I ever planned to do either. But, for an addict or alcoholic, driving under the influence is often a common occurrence. Sadly, an addicted person does many things that they never intended to do and they often *don't do* many things that they fully *intend* to do. Addiction robs us of ourselves in every way possible.

Maybe I felt that I was special and that nothing like a DUI arrest would ever happen to *me*. Then one night, after a business dinner with Xerox and many, many drinks the unthinkable did happen. Driving several colleagues back to their hotel, I found those red lights flashing in my rear view mirror. Still assuming there was no way they would give me a ticket, much less arrest me, I began my best sales pitch. But, the officer wasn't buying. I was angry and indignant, then sorry and apologetic. One minute I was threatening, then the next I was begging for mercy. I even told them that I would sue for false arrest because the prescription medication I was taking was making it worse. They agreed and immediately ordered a blood test to go with the breathalyzer test. That resulted in my being charged with driving under the influence of alcohol *and* prescription drugs.

I spent the night in an Orange County jail wondering how did this happen to a girl like me? I wasn't thinking of all that *could* have happened that night. I could have hurt or killed someone. No, I was only thinking about myself and how unfair this was to *me*. I awoke in the jail cell in an expensive business suit with torn stockings from the field sobriety test. I had never felt more humiliated. This was the absolute worse thing that had ever happened to me. At least it was the worst thing that had ever happened to me *so far*.

A few weeks later, I went to the courthouse for my official court date. I remember getting in line for traffic violations and when it was my turn, the lady behind the traffic window said something like, "This window is for *traffic* violations. You have committed a crime." Then she emphasized, "Drunk driving is a crime." After she repeated the word, *crime,* for the second time, I started thinking about what a mean woman she was. Come to think of it, she kind of reminded me of Mrs. Gulch in the first scene of the Wizard of Oz. She was just like that mean lady who was trying to take Toto from Dorothy to have him "destroyed."

I was ordered to pay thousands of dollars in fines and sentenced to a DUI class. The class was interesting. The instructor in my DUI class was a recovering alcoholic and made a shocking statement at the beginning of the first class. He said that statistically only two of you, in a class of thirty or so, are *not* alcoholic. I was shocked by that assertion. He went on to explain the data showing how many times people drive drunk before they are actually arrested for drunk driving. Statistically speaking, he said, "Most of us are alcoholic." I remember looking around the room and saying to myself, "Me and that guy over there are not alcoholics." Well, it turns out, as in so many things in my life, I was wrong. Thinking about it now, I was probably wrong about that guy in the corner as well.

Many years later, in early recovery, I heard this speaker at a large convention in San Francisco who was talking about when he first got sober. He described a night when he had been out drinking and couldn't remember how he got home. He had been so drunk the night before that he could not remember if he drove home or took a taxi. So the next morning, he went downstairs to check to see if his car was in the garage. As he walked into the garage, he was shocked to discover that his car was indeed parked in its usual spot, but looking for his car on this particular morning wasn't like all the others. You see, this morning he found a dead body lying on the hood of the car. He had killed someone driving home drunk the night before and had simply gone up to bed to sleep off a stupor, never even realizing what he had done. That was his first day of his sobriety and he went on to spend many years in prison.

When I heard that story I thought about how many times I, too, had gone out into *my* garage the morning after a night out drinking with friends. Like this man, I had gone looking to see if I had driven home the night before. Many times I found my garbage can smashed up against the door or the wall. Once I found the car smashed into the garage refrigerator, which still has the dent today. On another occasion, the entire garbage can was on top of my car.

A chill ran through me as I sat in that meeting long ago and realized for the first time that his story could have easily been *my* story. "But for the grace of God, there go I" is a saying my 12-Stepping friends use all the time and I knew that, but for the grace of God, I could have been this man. I began to feel grateful that I had been handcuffed that night in October of 1987. I was, for the first time, grateful that I had been humiliated and punished because ultimately, I was saved from hurting or killing someone that night and on so many other nights.

In the movie, the Wizard of Oz, Gilda kept showing up right when Dorothy was in big trouble. She would show up as a bright light or a beautiful floating bubble, but she was always there when Dorothy really needed her. God has surely watched over me every moment of my life. He has protected me, even from myself.

Recently, I was the keynote speaker at for a large 12-Step recovery speaker meeting and the man who had killed someone sought me out to say that he was the man in my story. He was so grateful to know that his story was making a difference.

Today, as a Law Enforcement Chaplain in Sacramento County, I often work at DUI checkpoints in different communities. I'm amazed at the journey that God is taking me on. I've seen how He is able to use some of my biggest mistakes in life to help others get better. One day I'm sitting with a mom who is being arrested for drunk driving who is sure it's the end of the world. Next, I'm talking to a veteran who has become homeless in his alcoholism. Daily, I've been witness to how God can turn our really big and bad mistakes into messages of hope and recovery.

Over the years, I've been blessed by the opportunity to be with all kinds of people in all kinds of crises. I've rushed to the hospital to be with the family of a police officer killed in the line of duty and I've stood by the road all night with the mother whose son has just been gunned down by a rival gang. It is in the bad times that we *know* we *need* God. He seems to whisper to us during the good times and He shouts to us during adversity. I've known adversity and I know His power to save. But, I'm getting ahead of myself. Let me tell you more about the tornado I survived.

As my prescription addiction progressed, the time quickly came when I simply could not continue working. Leaving Xerox Corporation was just like leaving the University of Arkansas. If I couldn't be the very best at something, I generally didn't want to do it at all. So, whatever the situation, I would leave on some pretense of having something better than what they were offering. I had loved that job, but it was simply impossible for me to do in my addicted state. Giving it up allowed me to finally and completely lose myself in the addiction.

My life was spiraling out of control. After quitting my job, my whole existence became about using prescriptions. From the moment I woke up, all through the day and night, I was chasing that high. I began to run a drug fever, which is a low-grade, persistent fever caused by the chronic use of narcotics. I was hospitalized to determine the source of the fever and of course, as always, to treat the pain.

During one of those hospitalizations I had a grand mal seizure caused by an overdose of Demerol. My tolerance for the drug was so high that I could take massive quantities of opiates. Can you imagine overdosing on Demerol while in the hospital? All of the Demerol was being administered by the hospital and yet it never occurred to me that I could die. I just knew that I needed the drug. And I needed *more* of it every day, a *lot* more.

I remember the day of the overdose well. A nurse came into my room to give me another shot of Demerol through the IV. Even though I was on round the clock Demerol, she said they were giving me an extra big shot because I was going to be transported to another hospital for some tests. She said they wanted to make sure that I was out of pain for some time. I thought that sounded like a really good idea. I watched as she put the syringe filled with Demerol into the IV and I watched the drug slowly enter the tubing. Then, I watched the medication enter my body. I *loved* this process and always made a point of watching *every* move the medication made. I watched that precious fluid from the moment it left the vial and was put inside the syringe, to when the syringe was placed in my IV, to when the nurse began squeezing the liquid into the tubing, and finally, I watched the Demerol as it entered my body. I loved the burning sensation as the medication entered my arm and the rush of euphoria as that precious fluid joined my blood and flowed through the veins in my body. I loved the floating feeling as it reached my brain and, in that moment, all was right with the world.

On this day, however, something tragic happened. As I started to feel the medication affecting my body, I suddenly lost consciousness. I had never lost consciousness before. I awoke with the taste of blood in my mouth and blood on the front of my hospital gown. My head was throbbing and felt like someone was hitting me with a hammer. There were two doctors and several nurses in my room, all of them working frantically. I was told that I had had a grand mal seizure and that they had almost lost me. After the seizure, they decided to do another series of tests. But, what I really wanted to know was, "When could I receive the next pain shot?"

They rescheduled the MRI for the next day. I remember the nurse telling me before that MRI that if they did not find anything on this brain scan, they would have to consider the possibility that all of these drugs could be the cause of my problems. As she said those words to me, I felt a fear like I had never known in my entire life.

In thinking back, that nurse was just another Mrs. Gulch in my life, always trying to steal something from me or destroy something I loved and needed. After she left the room, I remember praying a prayer that only an addicted person could understand. I said, "Please God, let them find something on that brain scan." I know that sounds crazy, but it was the honest prayer I muttered that day. At that point, I would rather have had them find a brain tumor on that MRI and tell me that I had six months to live, than to hear them say that the drugs were the problem. I couldn't imagine it if they were to tell me that my *solution*, pain medications, was the *problem*. To suggest that I needed to stop taking these drugs was inconceivable to me! It was never going to happen! I would not let it happen! I would run to the ends of the earth, like Dorothy trying to save Toto, I would do anything to save this thing that I loved and needed!

In 12-Step recovery, the second step says, "Came to believe that a Power greater than ourselves could restore us to sanity." Yet, when I came into 12-Step recovery many years later, I had a real problem with that step. The God part didn't bother me; it was the insanity part that had me stumped. I fully believed that I had never been insane, even knowing that a sane person would never have prayed such a prayer as I had prayed from that hospital bed. Thankfully, God answered that prayer for me. He simply said, "No."

My recovery journey has been like an onion with many layers being peeled back over time and I'm grateful for passages like Ecclesiastes 3:1, *"To every thing there is a season, and a time to every purpose under the heaven."* God reveals to me exactly what I need in His perfect timing.

My mom flew up from southern California the night I had the grand mal seizure. I know today that if she hadn't come into town, I probably would not have survived the next 24 hours. She found me in the hospital room digging through my purse for pill bottles. I was screaming at her to leave me alone. Perhaps for the first time ever, I wanted her to get out of my life because, even in my drug-induced state, I knew she was talking to the doctors about all the prescriptions I was taking. She was working against me. Her instincts told her that something was *very wrong* and the truth is, long before the doctors were able to say these words to me, it was my mother who was speaking truth to everyone. She was saying, in fact yelling, "Michele is *addicted* to these prescriptions and they are going to kill her!" After she told them what she found me taking on my own, they rescheduled the MRI again. The doctor told my mom that if they had run those tests with all those drugs in my system that day, I would have died during the procedure.

After the drug fever, the constant headaches, and the grand mal seizure, the doctors ran every appropriate medical test. When they had ruled everything else out, the discussion turned again to the possibility that the prescriptions were likely the problem. The day I'd been dreading was upon me.

The doctors came in to announce that the prescriptions were possibly causing my headaches, and even the fever. They explained the concept of rebound headaches and told me about the drug fevers. As they talked the winds from the tornado seemed to blow faster and I felt completely hopeless.

They told me I needed to *slow down* my use of narcotic medications. They *did not tell me to stop* using them. No one at the hospital that day told me exactly *how* to slow down my use of narcotics. No one mentioned addiction or alcoholism to me. Certainly nobody suggested that I go to a 12-Step meeting or through a rehabilitation facility. No one told me anything about my problem. They just told me to slow down my use of narcotics and to only use them if I really needed them. I *needed* them everyday. I needed them many times throughout the day. It was a fact that I had real pain without the narcotics. What the doctors suggested sounded so foreign to me. It was as if they were asking me to live in a world without oxygen and only breathe air every now and then. Only breathe air when I really needed it? It was an impossible request.

Of course, I know today that the doctors and the HMO were protecting themselves. Prescription addicts are often on their own to find solutions to the problem, if they don't die first. The medical community is not quick to tell you that you are addicted to something that they gave you.

Still, being a people-pleaser and all, I thought I'd give it the old college try. So, I really tried to slow down my use of narcotics and to only use them when I absolutely needed them. I thought, "Come on Michele, you are a smart and capable girl. You can do this. I mean, how hard could this be? Right? Willpower, that's what I need. Willpower has always served me well in everything I tried to accomplish in life. I can do this."

Turns out, slowing down my use of prescription narcotics, was a bit tougher than I had anticipated. I would wake up sick and tell myself that I will just take two pills, every four hours, as prescribed, and every time it would go downhill from there. Because they were watching me now, very quickly I started doctor shopping to get what I truly needed. For the first time, I began lying to the doctors to get what I needed. I would go to emergency rooms in different parts of town to get Demerol shots, so they wouldn't remember me from the day before. I was in deep trouble and falling fast. I was no longer trying to be honest or seeking real solutions to my problems.

At one point, I realized that the doctors were more willing to continue to prescribe medications if they could *see* the pain I was in. So, I started rubbing my eye to make it red and inflamed. When they could see the pain they would prescribe basically limitless medications. I knew I was being dishonest with the doctors just as I had been with both of my families growing up. The shame of my duplicity was making my addiction darker and more deadly by the day. It seemed as if God was nowhere to be found. I was completely and utterly powerless over the addiction at that point.

I was eventually in such a bad place that I would do anything to convince the doctors to give me drugs. I remember a time when I sat crying on the bathroom floor, trembling and needing chemical help so badly. I thought if I only had an injury that would force them to give me drugs. So, I sat on my knees on the bathroom floor and started banging my head against the counter. I banged my head over and over again until it was bleeding and swollen. Then I called a friend to say that I had fallen and needed to go to the emergency room. Finally, hours later, I was given the much needed narcotic pain medications. I could float away again, at least for a few hours.

When the drugs wore off, I would be shaking so violently that I would have to take a few shots of alcohol just to stop the shaking. Most days I would drink alcohol just to seem normal enough to go see the doctor. He had the prescription drugs I needed most. My addiction was so far progressed at that point that I needed to set up my pills by the bedside before passing out. I knew I would be too sick and shaking too much to get it together when I awoke.

Honestly, I didn't know how to make it stop. I had always been a person who accomplished what I set out to do. I had big plans to turn my life around. I made long to-do lists and carried fancy organizers, but I never seemed to get anything accomplished and I couldn't understand why. Now, I was unable to even finish a simple project much less overcome a deadly addiction. It was during this period that I began to really hate being me. I seemed to be sinking deeper and deeper into a pit of despair. I was resentful and angry most of the time. I had become a victim and the victorious me had simply died.

Certainly, after the addiction to prescriptions, my feelings of failure and inadequacy were compounded. As an addicted person I was a disappointment to everyone and most especially to myself. My outward behavior was starting to match my deepest inward feelings. I would say I'd be there for you or that I would help with some project, but nine times out of ten, I would not show up. I was nowhere near following scripture like James 12:5 *"Let your 'yes' be yes and your 'no' be no."* I missed almost everything during the years of 1988-1990. I was hopelessly lost in a self-centered cycle of destruction.

Like Dorothy, I was usually left sitting on my bed watching the scenes of my life pass me by on the walls of the monster tornado. I missed birthday parties, funerals, holidays, family gatherings and so much more. Day after day, I'd sit in a drugged-out, anesthetized state, missing every aspect of life, the good and the bad.

My prescription addiction had become a large, Category 5 tornado. It had me in its grips, throwing me around. It was wiping out my whole life and destroying the hopes and dreams of my family as well. I knew at that point how powerless I was over this monster which had me in its grips. I knew also, I would not likely come out of this alive.

Chapter Three

Not in Kansas Anymore

The moment Dorothy stepped out of the black and white house from Kansas into the colorful world of Oz, we all knew that everything was different. She had landed in a dreamland. Every young person watching that movie for the first time can remember that scene. "We're not in Kansas anymore," said Dorothy. No truer words were ever spoken.

So it is with addiction. Once a person becomes addicted, everything in the world changes for them. Nothing is as it once was. Everything looks and feels, even tastes and smells different. The addiction tornado suddenly swept me up, ripped my life apart, and then dropped me into a foreign land. Stepping out of a normal life and into the life of addiction was as strange as that scene in the movie.

Every addicted person knows the peace and serenity of

the drug's effect. Our lives revolve around chasing that feeling of exhilaration and intoxication. Personal goals, ambitions, hopes and dreams; even our most precious relationships with friends and family all take a backseat to maintaining that drug euphoria. It becomes the master. The drugs take precedence over everything in life and nothing matters more than the addiction.

I remember when people would say, "Why don't you just stop, you have so much going for you?" I would think, are they crazy? Why can't they see that the whole world has changed and we're not in Kansas anymore?

While there might have been excitement in the beginning, the story continues. Dorothy's yearning to go home is the same profound longing of every alcoholic. We are lost and pining to get back to that place of normalcy, home. Just as with Dorothy in the Land of Oz, getting back to that place seems to be an impossible task.

I'm so grateful that my family never gave up on me and in 1990 they intervened and put me in the Care Unit in Orange County, California. They were at a complete loss of how to help me, so they reached out to professionals in the area of addiction and alcoholism. At the time, I was angry. Over the next few weeks, I went through an incredibly difficult detoxification coming off all those prescription narcotics. The doctor at the Care Unit told me I had been in their PCU (Primary Care Unit) for longer than any patient he could remember in their facility, including all the patients coming off illegal or street drugs. I was a very sick person.

The fact that my detoxification had been more difficult than the other patients in the Care Unit wasn't shocking to me at all. I knew I was in really bad shape. I suffered through their medical detoxification, shaking, vomiting and even hallucinating. There were nights in that Care Unit when I was certain that I would die. I was incredibly weak. The medical staff would assure me that this would pass, but still, it was scary. One night I woke up in the dark room and could see several giant spiders climbing up the wall in front of my bed. I reached down and picked up a shoe and threw it as hard as I could at those spiders. Within minutes, the nurses came running in and, with the lights on, I could see that there was nothing there. Those first few days in detox, I felt vulnerable and frightened most of the time.

A doctor at that Care Unit explained to me that, in his medical opinion, I was an alcoholic. I remember telling him that I was absolutely *not* an alcoholic; I just had this little problem with doctors and prescription drugs. I sat there in my hospital gown and slippers and expressed complete indignation at his silly suggestion that I was an alcoholic. I told him in no uncertain terms that there was no way that was possible. I was definitely *not* an alcoholic.

At the Care Unit, patients were required to go to 12-Step meetings everyday. Many 12-Step meetings were held at their facility and it was there that I was first introduced to 12-Step recovery. I would go shuffling into those first 12-

Step recovery meetings with all of the other patients doing what recovery friends called the "Thorazine shuffle." Thorazine is a detoxification drug which makes your legs feel like they weigh a thousand pounds, so the drug made it hard to lift your feet and walk normally. I would shuffle in, sit down, and try to listen to what they were saying. Although, I must say, listening was especially hard in my condition.

Still, I was sincerely moved by those 12-Step support group meetings. The people shared so much about their broken lives. I thought these were wonderful groups and I was really happy that *they* had these groups because clearly, *these* people *really needed* them. Those 12-Steppers seemed to genuinely love and support each other. From their personal stories, it was clear that they were alcoholics and really needed this type of group therapy. It seemed to be working for them because they did appear to be happy, joyous and free from their addictions.

The overachiever and people pleaser in me took over as I attempted to be the best in my recovery class of patients in that Care Unit. I read the 12-Steps on the wall in those meeting halls and I thought those looked like a pretty good idea. I thought I'd do those steps and I'd do them better than anyone had ever done them before. Honestly, God met me right where I was at that Care Unit. He used my character defects of people pleasing and ego to teach me something about myself. It was something that I couldn't possibly understand right then, but something I would need to know about my problem later on. Remember how Dorothy walked around with the Ruby Shoes on her feet and she didn't understand the power of the gift she'd be given? That was me at the Care Unit – naive, pretending, searching, and like everyone else, just wanting to go home.

So, I sat in my hospital room one afternoon and I read their 12-Steps. Then, I shuffled back to a meeting and announced to the group that I had worked the steps on my own and just needed someone to listen to a few things on Step 5 and then I was done. The funny thing is that when I made that announcement, I really thought they would be proud of me. Maybe they would be impressed by my initiative. Perhaps I was the first person *ever* to complete the 12-Steps so quickly. But, those 12-Steppers just smiled at me and said, "Keep coming back, Honey." They hadn't responded at all the way I had thought they would respond. They didn't seem impressed by me even a little bit. While I didn't think they were making fun of me, on the contrary, I felt that they loved me all the more. I was confused by those 12-Stepping friends.

Soon, I started attending a book study, mostly, again, because I wanted to be the best at whatever I was doing. I read and critiqued their book and their teaching styles. I did personal assessments of these teams of volunteer 12-Steppers. Who were these people really? What motivated them to behave as they did?

In those early book studies and step studies, I began to learn some things about the disease of alcoholism. Not that it related to me, but here again, God was using my character defects to teach me something that I didn't know. I mean what kind of a person, who's not an alcoholic, sits and studies "The Big Book of Alcoholics Anonymous"? So, pretending to be a part of it all, the people pleaser in me kept studying their literature.

I learned that an alcoholic has an allergy of the body which causes a physical craving once the body has been altered by a mind altering substance of any kind. They call this the *phenomenon of craving*. They mentioned also the *mental obsession* of the alcoholic mind. The alcoholic has a mind that tells him over and over again throughout his lifetime, that he doesn't have this problem. The alcoholic has a brain that is constantly telling him that maybe this time, things will be different. They also mentioned the *spiritual malady* of every alcoholic. When they talked about the malady, I thought to myself, you're kidding me, right? You guys are going to tell *me* about God? I'd spent my whole life in church and in Bible studies. I could teach them a thing or two about God. They probably didn't even know all the books of the Bible. Please!

After all the study, I was more convinced than ever that I was *not* an alcoholic. I just had a problem with doctors and prescription drugs and I was never going to do anything like that again. I mean I wasn't a crazy person. I had just been through a terribly difficult detox. I was about sixty days off of all those prescriptions, the hallucinations and shaking had finally stopped, and I was never going to do that again. Not ever.

One day after leaving the Care Unit, I went with a group of friends who were going down to a local restaurant and bar to have a few drinks. I thought I would come along. I mean what could it hurt, right? I had been out of detox for more than two months and certainly I would never go back to prescriptions. I might have a drink, if I felt like it, but I knew that I was done forever with doctors and drugs.

Just as those 12-Steppers had predicted when I left treatment, after having a few margaritas, everything changed. That tornado, which had quieted down during detox, suddenly began howling again with a fiery force and strong, unpredictable winds. Within six hours I was back getting IV Demerol from my "doctor feel good."

I woke up the next morning and thought, how did this happen to me? I never intended to take Demerol. I remember thinking about what they had told me at those book studies. I remember them talking about the physical craving and how the alcoholic is powerless once they take that dreaded first drink. That morning was the first time I ever considered the remote possibility that I might, in fact, be an alcoholic. The words of that recovery doctor rang in my ears, but the craving was back and I couldn't stop. Taking that first drink was my big mistake.

In the coming months, as my prescription addiction grew, my family intervened again, and put me back into another detox facility, this time in the Sacramento area at a place called Starting Point. At inpatient recovery facilities, they go through all your bags and search for drugs, alcohol, and all the things you are not supposed to bring into a recovery facility. My family took my wallet and money, hoping that I would stay and get better. But, I was nowhere near ready to surrender. By this time, I was just angry and felt victimized by everything and everyone. No one understood how I felt. They were all against me.

Before my family handed me over to Starting Point, I stuck a credit card in the lining of my luggage. I had an escape route. Within a few days, I called a taxi to come pick me up from Starting Point. I remember getting into the taxi and telling the driver to take me to a liquor store and then to a pharmacy. He laughed and said something like, "I've never picked up someone from Starting Point and taken them to a liquor store *and* a pharmacy before." I didn't think he was funny and come to think of it, if Mrs. Gulch had a husband in the story, he would surely have looked like this loser guy.

After I picked up all that I needed to feel "normal" again, alcohol and what my 12-Stepping friends call lumpy alcohol (prescriptions), I asked the driver to leave me at the Oxford Suites in Roseville, California. I checked in, and then quite literally, I checked out. The next thing I knew, I woke up in an emergency room of a Roseville hospital with blood on my shirt, tubes down my throat, and the taste of charcoal in my mouth *once again*. Apparently, the taxicab driver had alerted authorities that something was wrong. Thank God he did!

I never intended to overdose; I was just trying to feel normal again. Once I started prescriptions, I never seemed to stop. The doctors in the hospital told me that I would have died had they not pumped out my stomach that day. That obnoxious taxicab driver turned out to be my very own "taxi angel" intervening on my behalf. I know that God was all around me during that dark time. Just as Glinda would appear out of nowhere to help Dorothy, waving her sparkly wand, God was, *in a very real sense*, taking care of me because, at that point, I was surely unable to care for myself.

My brain had been completely fried by all the drugs. And it was getting worse by the day. After I was out of one of those spin dry places, I had an appointment with a recovery doctor downtown. I remember standing in front of a parking meter completely confused about what to do next. I had separated in my hand nickels on one side and quarters on the other side. I knew they were different coins, but I could not determine which one worked in the parking meter. I stopped a man on the street and asked him which one would go in the parking meter. He looked at me with complete amazement. Was I kidding? Was I mentally ill? He wasn't sure, but he took pity on me. He picked up a quarter out of my hand and placed it in the meter for me. He told me to put the nickels away because they would not work in the parking meters and he walked away.

On other occasions, I would sit at stoplights and try to remember which one meant go and which one meant stop. Sometimes I would sit at a green light too long and then someone would honk at me. Many drivers would get angry or frustrated and drive around me. Then I would remember that green meant go. My brain had been severely damaged by prescription addiction.

I had double vision for a long time and could read very little. In early recovery, when I had to read, I would often hold my hand over one eye. It took me months to be able to read normally again. My mind couldn't focus, and even after the double vision had stopped, my comprehension of written words seemed to have vanished.

I kept trying to figure out how and why this had happened to me. I kept trying to find some way to get back to normal, back to Kansas and home. As I discussed my dilemma and my frustrations with my new 12-Stepping friends, a wise, old lady just smiled at me and said, "Honey, once you're a pickle, you'll never be a cucumber again." What a simple way of explaining the complexities of alcoholism to a confused and hopeless person like me. I realized for the first time, I was a pickle and would never be a normal cucumber again. I would never be the same person ever again. Everything about me had changed. It didn't matter how I became pickled or even what kind of pickle I was; sweet, dill, or bread and butter. I needed to begin to accept my pickleness and stop trying to be a cucumber again. Finding my way home, she explained, would be all about my *surrender* and my complete acceptance of who I was now.

I began to wonder; perhaps I would never go home again. Perhaps I was lost in this strange place forever. But, one thing I knew for sure, if I ever made it home again, I would be a completely different person when I arrived.

Part Two: Recovery – My Way

Chapter Four

Slipping Away - Over the Rainbow

Perhaps one of the most familiar songs in the world is "Somewhere Over the Rainbow," sung by Judy Garland in 1939. This magnificent song inspires people to hope that someday, somehow, or somewhere, things will get better. It is both sad and ironic that Judy Garland died at the young age of 47 of a prescription drug overdose. Judy Garland was young, beautiful, and talented. She did not have to die this way. She gave hope to others in the lyrics she sang. Why couldn't she find that hope for herself?

The song, "Somewhere Over the Rainbow," concedes a kind of hopelessness as well and we all feel it on some level. Life is hard and even when things are good; you know that someday, there will be trouble again. Perhaps Judy Garland was as lost as I was. Maybe she was singing about her desire to get back home and could never find her way back.

The way I see it, "Somewhere Over the Rainbow" could be the alcoholic's theme song. We understand feeling sad, hopeless and yet hopeful all at the same time. For an addicted person, "Somewhere Over the Rainbow" perfectly describes our dilemma. We are stuck in a black and white world and we are looking for color. We are looking for a place where there are no troubles. In fact it is a place where "troubles melt like lemon drops." How cool would that be?

Look closely at the lyrics of this timeless song:

> *Somewhere, over the rainbow, way up high.*
> *There's a land that I heard of once in a lullaby.*
> *Somewhere, over the rainbow, skies are blue.*
> *And the dreams that you dare to dream really do come true.*
> *Someday I'll wish upon a star and wake up*
> *where the clouds are far behind me.*
> *Where troubles melt like lemon drops, away above the chimney*
> *tops, that's where you'll find me.*
> *Somewhere, over the rainbow, bluebirds fly.*
> *Birds fly over the rainbow,*
> *Why then - oh, why can't I?*
> *If happy little bluebirds fly beyond the rainbow,*
> *Why, oh, why can't I?*

So let me get this straight. We are talking about a place where the dreams we dare to dream really do come true. A place way above the chimney tops where troubles melt like lemon drops. And, this is also a place beyond the rainbow where happy little bluebirds fly. I share Dorothy's question, why then, oh why can't I?

The truth is that Demerol took me there. Demerol and lots of other mind altering prescription drugs *always* took me, and Judy Garland, over the rainbow. Like no other experience I have ever known, prescription medications, can instantly transport me to that happy place, "Over the Rainbow." And they can take me there anytime I choose to go.

The problem is, and this is a *very* important distinction, just like in the movie, it is a *make-believe place*. I can visit there, in a dreamlike state, but I can never really *live* there. The euphoria wears off and I am left in a darker and more desperate world than ever before. Each time I travel to and from that place, I am even more lost than the last time I returned. Home gets farther and farther away from me.

My sponsor in recovery is a truly gifted speaker. Robin often speaks at conventions and other large meetings. She always closes her talks with the Promises from "The Big Book of Alcoholics Anonymous." However she reads this passage a little differently. So that you will be familiar with the Promises, let me share them with you. They are found after the Ninth Step in "The Big Book of Alcoholics Anonymous."

"We are going to know a new freedom and a new happiness. We will not regret the past nor wish to shut the door on it. We will comprehend the word serenity and we will know peace. No matter

how far down the scale we have gone, we will see how our experience can benefit others. That feeling of uselessness and self-pity will disappear. We will lose interest in selfish things and gain interest in our fellows. Self-seeking will slip away. Our whole attitude and outlook upon life will change. Fear of people and of economic insecurity will leave us. We will intuitively know how to handle situations which used to baffle us. We will suddenly realize that God is doing for us what we could not do for ourselves. Are these extravagant promises? We think not. They are being fulfilled among us - sometimes quickly, sometimes slowly. They will always materialize if we work for them."

Most 12-Steppers know the Promises well. For obvious reasons, they are a cherished reading in many different 12-Step programs. In essence, they are a series of Promises that suggest that if we stay on the path of recovery, we will all eventually make our way back home.

Robin closes by reading the Promises something like this:

When I drank, I knew a new freedom and a new happiness.

When I drank, I did not regret the past nor wish to shut the door on it.

When I drank, I could comprehend the word serenity and I knew peace.

When I drank, no matter how far down the scale I had gone I could see how my experience could benefit others.

When I drank, that feeling of uselessness and self-pity would disappear.

When I drank, my whole attitude and outlook on life would change.

When I drank, I intuitively knew how to handle situations which used to baffle me.

Robin knew that what I was always looking for in that bottle of pills or in that bottle of alcohol was *exactly* what I would find in 12-Step recovery. It is what I believe Judy Garland was singing about in "Somewhere Over the Rainbow." She was looking for some make-believe place as a *substitution* for the home which she, and I, could no longer find.

"Somewhere Over the Rainbow" is a rip-off and not even a *real* live place to live. It will *never* be home for any of us. But, my ability to check out of this world and go "Over the Rainbow" *is* very real. With a little pharmaceutical help, I can choose to fly away anytime. Just as Dorothy knew she couldn't stay in the Land of Oz, I knew that I could never live there either. And the higher I flew, the farther I got from home.

Living our lives "Over the Rainbow" is a lonely and dangerous idea. Judy Garland's short life reminds me of how perilous it really is to live a make-believe life. No matter how rich or famous or successful a person is, living a life of pretense through prescription drug addiction will always end badly. How many stars have we seen fall? Michael Jackson, Whitney Houston, Elvis Presley, Heath Ledger, River Phoenix, John Belushi, Marilyn Monroe, and this list could go on and on. The sad truth is that it didn't have to end this way.

Prescriptions can sneak up on anyone. They are not social drugs. No one goes out to a bar to have a few "prescriptions." Usually, they are done *alone* at home. It is a private and lonely addiction. Prescriptions are generally taken for a very real medical condition, at least in the beginning. Most people are caught off guard by prescription addiction. As a Law Enforcement Chaplain, I see all types of people addicted to prescriptions. Police Officers, for example, generally start with a legitimate injury, but sometimes end up with a much bigger problem. Many will spend the rest of theirs lives trapped and enslaved by a prescription addiction. Doctors, nurses, even clergy and other professionals are often seduced by the clinical and benign nature of prescribed medications that lure you to sleep only to awaken you to a nightmare that many will never escape.

Judy Garland could have felt many of the same feelings I did; maybe she felt lost, alone, and hopeless. I'll bet she was longing to go *home,* too. Maybe, Judy Garland's constant prayer was just like mine and Dorothy's from the Land of Oz. Maybe she kept saying to God, "I've got to get back home. Please help me get back home." Maybe in the end, she discovered the truth that the drug euphoria of "Somewhere Over the Rainbow" was just a make-believe place and the drugs had let her down as well.

I'll never know if Judy Garland's experiences with prescriptions and this beautiful song were like mine. Still, I wish I could introduce her to my friend, Robin. I wish Robin and I could sit with her, as we've sat with so many other women. Together, we'd read The Promises and help her see all we've learned about our deadly struggle with the prescription addiction tornado. I pray that Judy Garland finally found her way home, to a *real* home. I pray that we all do.

Chapter Five

The Emerald City

When Dorothy and her friends see the sparkling Emerald City in the distance, there is suddenly great joy and excitement. The group begins running through the colorful poppy fields toward the illusive Emerald City. Everyone in the Land of Oz had assured them that this was the place where they could finally get the help they needed. Lion would find courage, Tin Man would receive his heart, and the Scarecrow would finally obtain that brilliant brain he'd always wanted. Dorothy just hoped she might finally get to go home. The poppy field stops the group before they even arrive at the gates of the Emerald City.

This is how it was for me in early recovery. Many times I would start chasing a solution which was right before me. That solution would appear to be so easily attainable and I could finally see hope on the emerald horizon. Then, something would happen and, just like Dorothy, I'd find myself falling asleep in the poppy field. Those poisonous poppies would throw me a curveball every time. I'd start taking prescriptions again and drift away. I'd say to my friends, "I'm just going to sleep for a while." I'd tell myself that I just needed to take a break from life and rest for a while. Again and again, I returned to my addiction, deciding to sleep in the poppy field and put off life for another day.

Dorothy's faithful friends cried out for help from that poppy field. They prayed, "Please help Dorothy!" And once again, Glinda floated in as a bright pink balloon, full of radiance and love. The grace that Glinda provided Dorothy in the poppy field came in the form of snow falling so gently and breaking the wicked spell of the poppies. It reminded me of manna falling from heaven bringing lifesaving relief here on earth. Heavenly angels seem to always be floating above me. As distraught friends and family prayed for me during those perilous years, God's grace would always float in, as if on queue. It was manna from heaven falling upon me like snow in the poppy field.

My friends like to tease me by saying I had done a tremendous amount of "research and development" on the disease of alcoholism. Their meaning was that I suffered from chronic relapse which, of course, was true. It took me a great deal longer than most to accept my problem. Reluctantly, and very slowly, I started to accept the fact that they might be right about me. I might just be a prescription addict and maybe even an alcoholic, too. I had tried every trick in the book to manage or control my addiction. Willpower had failed me and things seemed to be getting worse by the day.

My real life "city of hope" was 12-Step meetings in early recovery. I finally made it through that deadly poppy field of everlasting sleep and arrived at the gates of the Emerald City. For the first time in my life, I ran to recovery, *not because someone was forcing me*, but because I realized *I needed help*. I checked *myself* into my third and final treatment center, New Dawn Recovery Center in Fair Oaks, California. I began to hope that maybe Oz was great and powerful enough to finally help me get back home. Everything was new and exciting.

At New Dawn, they had a morning ritual where the leader would ask each person to express, in a word or two, how they were feeling on that particular morning. I could never think of what to say and would often consider the question prior to walking into group. Identifying and understanding feelings was a skill I had never learned. I was amazed at how so many people could easily find the words to express *exactly* how they were feeling at any given moment.

I had grown up stuffing those feelings and taking prescriptions helped me escape. Growing up in the south might have complicated things a bit, too. I mean every good southern family understands the importance of the "look good." Don't get me wrong, I *love* the south and most especially, I love southern people. I am one. My southern friends have been blessed with the gift of hospitality, love, and service, like *nowhere* else in the world. But in my experience, honestly assessing one's feelings and *actually talking about it with a group of strangers* isn't exactly a southern specialty.

For the most part, feelings were useless in my world. They generally got in the way of one's effectiveness. I had no idea how to share my feelings because I had no idea how to *identify* my feelings. I never thought much about how I felt about anything. Although, I'd certainly spent a great deal of time guessing about what others might be feeling about me. When it came to feelings, I just numbed them with medications, alcohol, or even food.

So the recovery house leaders decided that I needed some extra help and they gave me a "feelings chart" to move me along. I was the only one with a cheat sheet in my recovery support group. My "feelings chart," which I had to bring with me every morning, was filled with happy and sad faces. Next to the face was a long list of possible feelings. I used my "feelings chart" everyday for many months to help me start identifying how I felt. I began to understand the difference of when I felt anxious, or overwhelmed, or grateful, or fearful, or accomplished. It was a really cool new skill.

Today, I know that while feelings aren't facts,

understanding how I feel about my circumstances in life can help me see my motivations more clearly. Learning this little skill has helped me understand more about myself. Then, I was on my way to developing what I'd call, "advanced recovery skills," like knowing that the way I feel about the people in my life, and specifically, the way I feel about God is a *mirrored reflection* of how I feel about *myself* at any given moment in time.

In case you missed it, yes, that's right, the academic scholar had to use a cheat sheet to help her along. Most of my "character assets" coming into recovery have turned out to be some of my greatest liabilities. Dr. Lackner, a wonderful friend and recovery doctor, used to tell me that a person can never be too dumb, too poor, or too ugly to get better in 12-Step recovery, but a person can be too smart, too rich, or too good looking to get better. I thought that was a funny thing to say, but it turns out he was exactly right. I have seen it over and over again. Many people die simply because they are too smart, or too rich, or too beautiful to really surrender and get better. They never fully accept the fact that they are a pickle and will never be a cucumber again.

One of my earliest recovery friends was a beautiful girl, inside and out. I remember staying up late at the recovery house with Maryanne, talking and laughing about everything under the sun. She lived in a huge, fancy home up in the hills with incredible views of Folsom Lake. Her family tried for years to help her get better, but in the end, Maryanne was perhaps too beautiful, too wealthy, and too smart to really surrender. It broke my heart when, after yet another relapse, she died in her exquisite four-post, mahogany bed high up above Folsom Lake. She drank herself to death.

After Maryanne died, I listened more intently when my 12-Stepping friends told me that I was always comparing my insides with everyone else's outsides. Although I'd never let you know it, I'd often be thinking I was better than you or worse than you. 12-Steppers say, "We are egomaniacs with inferiority complexes." Either way, this faulty, and maybe even narcissistic thinking, always left me *alone*. It left me alone at the top of the world or alone at the bottom of the world, but I was always alone. They said that I needed to learn to be a banana in the bunch. I needed to learn to be one among many.

During that time I met Johnny Z, a kind and gentle man, who is the love of my life. When I met him in June of 1991, he was this young and really fun, sober guy. We met at a campout where he fished along a river. At the time, John was almost 7 years sober, and I thought that sounded like forever. Having gotten sober at the young age of seventeen, John loved the 12-Step recovery life. He had such a good heart and seemed to be in constant service to others. He loved helping newcomers get started in 12-Step recovery. He was a small business employer and, subsequently he was able to employ people and even helped many start their own businesses or launch careers in the industry. He believed that 12-Step recovery wasn't just something he did to stay sober. For him it was a spiritual journey and new way of life. Johnny Z was one of the very first gifts my recovery life brought me and little did I know that the recovery gifts would just continue to multiply.

Inside the Emerald City of my early recovery, there was so much excitement. For the first time in a very long time life became *fun* again. Running around with Johnny Z and his crazy friends, going to conventions and conferences all over the country, I felt free and alive. We did dances, campouts, young people recovery functions, and so many other fun, sober activities.

You know the scene inside the Emerald City when Dorothy and her friends were getting all fixed up in preparation for a visit with the Wizard? That was exactly how I felt. For the first time in years, I was so excited and hopeful for my future. During that time, in the early 90's, my life began to get better. John and I were married in November 1993 and within a few years had two beautiful daughters. Sarah was born in 1995 and Katie was born in 1999. They were both miraculous answers to many, many prayers. The gifts just kept on coming. Our business grew, we bought a home, cars, a boat, we traveled the world and enjoyed the life that recovery was giving us.

I felt glamorous and hopeful about my future as

Dorothy and her friends did when they emerged from the beauty parlors within the Emerald City. They were picked up in carriages with horses which actually changed colors and to top it off, Dorothy and her friends were surrounded by cheering crowds. Life in the Emerald City was good and 12-Step recovery was a brand-new and exciting life for me. Everyday was another adventure, a new way of looking at things.

I don't want to give you the wrong impression. While early recovery was exciting and new, it wasn't *easy* for me. Recovery seemed easier for John and so many of our friends who had, long ago, fully surrendered their problem to God. But, for me, recovery came extremely slow and was much more difficult. I was still holding on to old ideas and attitudes. Others were able to accept this new way of life. Their lives seemed to model the recovery mottos; live and let live, one day at a time, easy does it, keep it simple, first things first, and so on. I'm sure that wasn't always true but, from the outside looking in, that's what I saw. By continuing to compare myself to others, I was setting myself up to fail. I was my own worst enemy.

I brought all my best coping skills into 12-Step recovery. I thought that I wasn't angry, but I was definitely a victim. I didn't know it then, but I had perfected the art of passive aggressive behavior. I was either your best friend or, if you hurt my sensitive feelings and I was mad at you, you might as well have been dead to me. The slightest disagreement in my marriage and I would go straight to my thinking that maybe this wasn't going to work out with John. I had a lot to learn about relationships and how to get along with others.

Do you remember the scene in the movie when the newness of the Emerald City had worn off and Dorothy and her friends were left in a hallway all dressed up, scared and begging for a chance to see the great and powerful Oz? I was eventually left there thinking about recovery. Is this really all there is and how *exactly* can this help me forever?

I once heard someone say that there are two types of people who come into recovery, those who are suicidal and those who are homicidal. I thought, oh good, because I'm not the homicidal and angry type. I'm more the type of person who is hard on myself. Surely, I must be better off. Then they explained that the suicidal alcoholic is much worse off because he doesn't even know he's angry yet. They said that anger and resentment is a secondary emotion and I hadn't even gotten that far yet. Why was this *so* hard for me?

To make matters worse, even in recovery, my headaches continued. In the mid-1990's I had as much as four years in recovery doing it *my way*. Then, I would try a new prescription drug that had just come on the market, thinking maybe *this* one will help me. Maybe, this time, it won't lead me back into the addiction tornado. The recovery phrase, *one is too many and a thousand never enough,* fit me perfectly. Once I took just one of anything, I was off and running. Each and every time, I would end up sleeping in the poppy field again.

Even when recovery friends cautioned me about *all* mind-altering medications, I would think, "Maybe *this time*, with *this medication*, it'll be different." I thought all those recovery rules didn't necessarily apply to *me*. Besides, I had *real* headaches. But, the result was always the same. Once I started taking any of those mind altering medications I was completely powerless to stop. Even if I was careful and started slowly, even if I took them as prescribed, I always ended up misusing them and my addiction would take off again. I had lost the power to choose and if I took one, the battle was lost.

With every dangerous relapse, I would drift farther away from home. In looking back my worsening relapses were described by Jesus in the cautionary passage in Matthew 12: 43-45, *"When an impure spirit comes out of a person, it goes through arid places seeking rest and does not find it. Then it says, 'I will return to the house I left.' When it arrives, it finds the house unoccupied, swept clean and put in order. Then it goes and takes with it seven other spirits more wicked than itself, and they go in and live there. And the final condition of that person is worse than the first."* The only way to keep from getting worse was to finally stop. I needed to find a way to make my empty dwelling place into a holy place that is filled with God. Of course, I had no idea how to accomplish something like that.

At that point, I had surrendered to the fact that I had a

problem, but deep down inside, I still felt maybe all this didn't apply to *me*. Maybe I thought I was different because when I first started coming around 12-Step meetings, I didn't really fit in anywhere. Prescription people really don't fit in any 12-Step program. I didn't feel like I belonged in Alcoholics Anonymous. They were nice people, but they drank too much and that wasn't really me. I just had a problem with doctors and drugs. I didn't belong in Narcotics Anonymous either. They were talking about drugs I had never even heard of before. I told myself that I didn't really fit in anywhere and isolated myself even from the very people trying to save me. I understood I had a problem with misusing prescriptions, but that was as far as I was willing to go.

Again, Dr. Lackner, the kind and gentle doctor from Sacramento, reminded me of a simple truth about myself. He said that I was just an alcoholic, plain and simple. He also said that because I thought I was *so* special, I could be a "terminally unique" case. He emphasized the word *terminally*. He told me as sternly as he possibly could that in his professional opinion, I was going to die of my terminal uniqueness. He suggested that I start looking for the *similarities* and not the differences in the experiences of my recovery friends. I really had no idea what he was talking about or even how to begin to follow his advice. At this point, I had only "token buy-in."

Sometimes in 12-Step meetings you hear people

identify as an alcoholic and an addict. My sponsor once told me how strange she thought that kind of statement was. She said, in her opinion, that statement was like saying, "I'm a German Shepherd and I'm a dog." She went on to say, "You may be a special *breed* of dog, Michele, I'll give you that, but until you accept your canine-ism you're not *ever* going to get better."

In my struggle with terminal uniqueness, I would say things like, "I haven't done *that* before and I would never do *that*." My recovery friends would say, "You haven't done that *yet!*" They loved to talk about the "yets." They even have an acronym for the word, *YETS* (You're. Eligible. Too. Silly.) Unfortunately, some of those "yets" had to happen to me before I could fully surrender and hear their words of caution.

Over the years, I've seen many people come and go in recovery. My husband and I have seen many friends relapse and die. Others relapsed and were sent to prison. You'd think that I would have been able to see where a life of untreated alcoholism and addiction would lead, but all of it didn't really apply to me because I was not like them. My mind kept telling me that my problems were different.

My early recovery life continued and I came in and out of 12-Step meetings. During that time, my medical insurance company decided that they weren't going to cover medical bills for my treatment of prescription addiction. That fact was especially troubling because I was facing some rather massive medical bills. I had an excellent medical plan through Xerox Corporation which included full coverage for the treatment of alcoholism and drug addiction. It would have covered me if I was trying to quit alcohol or even *illegal* drugs. Unfortunately, because I was coming off prescription medications, all of which they had prescribed, the decision was made not to cover the prescription addiction diagnosis. Perhaps they feared it would be an admission of some responsibility. Regardless of the reason, I was left holding the entire financial bag.

I tried for months to get the insurance company to help me. Finally, that kind doctor who had spoken truth to me early on recommended an attorney to intervene on my behalf. I remember telling the attorney to just ask the insurance company to pay for the medical bills. Getting those bills paid was really all that I cared about. Still, they refused to pay. Even after we filed a lawsuit, they refused to pay, only because my problem was with *prescription drugs*. We tried everything to get them to settle for the cost of the medical bills. Still, they refused.

Ultimately, the case went to arbitration and we won more than three times the amount of the medical bills. I am not a fan of lawsuits. That is why we tried so hard to get the insurance company to pay those medical bills, but they had refused to do the right thing.

After a couple of wobbly years in recovery, I was asked to speak to medical students at the University of California,

Davis about the problem of prescription addiction. The doctor and a professor at the university wanted me to share my personal experience in prescription drug addiction with the medical students.

Today, I understand the dilemma facing medical professionals who are treating prescription addicts. I know that doctors are in a quandary when it comes to treating a prescription addict. They can be in as much trouble for not prescribing narcotics to treat the pain an addict claims to have as they are for giving the addicted patient more narcotics. They seem to be in a no win situation. Subsequently, most doctors are forced to ignore prescription addicts, leaving the patient to find his or her own way out of this pit of destruction.

When I first started speaking to medical students, I was still angry that the doctors hadn't helped me earlier. I had little sympathy for the predicament they were in. I felt it was the medical profession's fault that I had this problem in the first place. I mean why did they start me on those shot cards in the beginning? Clearly, they didn't care about me. They cared more about their profits. I traveled to UC Davis on several occasions to speak with medical students. I knew they would someday be doctors and that they didn't choose the medical profession to *cause* problems for patients. They were going into this profession to *help* people, right? I hoped they would listen and care. I wanted to do what I could to make sure that what happened to me would not happen to others.

So, I decided to tell those medical students the truth. I explained to them that I blamed the doctors, the HMO, and the money saving efforts like shot cards for what had happened to me. I thought they had done this *to* me. I was determined to stop them and protect future victims from harm. I was finally getting angry. Unfortunately, I was just as lost as before. This time, I was lost in the Emerald City which turned out to be recovery done *my way*. It wasn't working.

On a positive note, after my case was concluded, and maybe because of the size of the judgment, this large HMO in California changed their entire policy regarding alcoholism and drug addiction treatment programs. Today, that organization has one of the very best recovery programs in our area. As a result of their policy changes, they now help thousands of addicted patients every year. Their recovery program today makes *no distinction* between alcohol, prescription or illegal drugs, which is a good thing. After all, we are "just dogs of a different breed."

Several years after my case was resolved, I had a friend contact me who worked for that large HMO. She knew of my case and the changes that resulted from my lawsuit. She told me that her job and the jobs of many other addiction specialists were not even around before my lawsuit. It had forced them to confront a problem. After my case, they began to look for better solutions for the patients they served. Looking back, I'm glad I followed that doctor's advice and talked to an attorney. I'm glad I stood up for myself by taking legal action against them. In the end, I know it has made a difference for many other patients in need of help.

All these years later, I'm honestly not resentful or angry with them anymore. In my recovery groups today, I see patients all the time coming in with cards to be signed from that HMO addiction program. After the meeting, when I sign those "meeting cards" for the newcomers, I feel gratitude beyond words. I'm grateful that I'm not holding a "shot card" and neither is this newcomer. I'm thankful that this large HMO is now giving out "meeting cards" *instead of* "shot cards" to patients. Mostly, I'm grateful for the recovery journey that we share today.

The Emerald City was a fictional place in the movie, "The Wizard of Oz." I think for me the Emerald City was my first recovery place. It was my introduction to a new way of life. Unfortunately, like Dorothy, I had no idea about how to actually live there. It certainly wasn't home. Like the fictional characters in the movie, the longer I was there, doing recovery "my way," the farther I was from home. I felt even more lost and hopeless with each passing day.

Chapter Six

Chasing Brooms

There was a great theologian from the 1500's named John Calvin who once said there are two important human tendencies with which every man struggles throughout his entire life. They are *tyranny* and *idolatry*. On the one hand I am tyrannically running the show, sure that the world would work better if everyone would just do things *my way*. I'll act like the great and powerful Oz controlling everything behind some façade. On the other hand, I struggle with *idolatry*, thinking maybe *this* will fix me and off I go again chasing the world's impossible brooms. In the Bible, the first two of the Ten Commandments are about *tyranny* and *idolatry*. The first commandment is *"You shall have no other gods before me."* Exodus 20:3. When I start running the show, I am actually playing God and breaking the first commandment. The second commandment is about *idolatry* which is putting something, anything, in front of God. *"You shall not make an idol."* Exodus 20:4.

Deep inside the Emerald City, Dorothy and her friends finally meet the Great and Powerful Oz. But, when they entered the ominous room to speak to the Wizard, he yelled at them through a fiery vale. If Oz was a savior, he was the ugliest and scariest savior to be found. The fire actually leapt when he screamed orders at them, "I am the great and powerful Oz!" I guess Oz didn't like being bothered with their silly requests. Perhaps, just to get them to go away, he finally told them, "I will grant your requests, but first you must prove yourselves worthy." He gave them an impossible and dangerous task. He said, "Go and get me the broom of the wicked witch!"

Like Dorothy, when I was new in recovery, I was angry that life seemed to be changing the rules on me. Still, Dorothy and I resigned ourselves to chasing brooms. Maybe Oz was right. Maybe that captured broom would prove my worthiness and would get me home.

One of the brooms I chased, as mentioned earlier, was changing the laws in the State of California. I wanted to make sure that no one ever fell into the deep hole of prescription addiction in which I had fallen. This was a broom I could capture. I was sure I could fix the problem. I started calling everyone I could think of who might be able to help me. I decided the shot cards the HMO had used had led to my addiction. They were the problem. Those shot cards had been the medical shortcut which had almost cost me my life. I was determined to make sure that narcotics were never distributed in this fashion to anyone ever again. I thought, if I could fix this, my life would be better. I would be *worthy* and maybe then I could get back home.

I spent a great deal of time with the State Medical Board and I got to know the leadership well. I also met with the Pharmaceutical Board on several occasions. I was resentful and determined. The head of the State Medical Board helped to encourage the legislation we ultimately proposed and passed. On a federal level, an agent with the Drug Enforcement Agency worked closely with me to affect change.

Assembly Bill 3260, a comprehensive omnibus medical bill, had taken about two years of my life. During the first few years of the 1990's shot cards and fighting that HMO became my crusade. Spending many long days and nights at the state capital, I was trying to capture the illusive broom which would surely save me. When AB 3260 was signed into law in 1992 with bipartisan support, I thought I had finally captured the witch's broom. Governor Pete Wilson signed my bill into law and the California Legislature had that signed law specially framed for me. That California law hangs in my office to this day and just like my college diploma, I can look at it, but it doesn't actually make me *feel* any different. It is just another broom in my quest to prove myself worthy of the great and powerful Oz's help. As I look around my office I find that the walls are covered with framed images of captured brooms, all sought in an effort to prove myself worthy.

Even after my bill became law, I continued to work with state and federal government agencies to affect change in the way prescription medications were dispersed in the State of California and across our country. I actually enjoyed much of the work I did and I know the changes in our laws were necessary and good. In recovery some say that when faced with any difficult situation you can always remember the acronym, A.C.E., accept, change, or eliminate. In every difficult situation, I have three options. I can either accept it, or change it, or I can work to eliminate it. In this case, I believed that the right thing to do was change it, so I did. Unfortunately, what I didn't realize at the time was that my motive in changing the law was more than simply making laws better for our citizens. *I also wanted something for me.* It was, unfortunately, something no law or government could give me.

Early in 1994, the Sacramento Bee published an article about my journey and several other media organizations picked up the story. For the next several months, I did numerous interviews, including radio, local news stations, and newspapers. Then I started hearing from national network news stations and programs like 60 Minutes and CBS Evening News.

On October 25th 1994, the CBS Evening News did a

national news story about my struggle with prescription addiction and everything changed for me that night. The special "Eye on America" segment was not only about my struggles with prescription medications, but about my efforts in changing the laws which made the addiction possible. When that program aired, I heard from people all across the country who were struggling with prescription addiction. I was overwhelmed and started to realize how vast and desperate the problem was for so many. I'd never realized how many people have the same problem with prescription addiction as I do. Today, because of my work in recovery, I am keenly aware of how vast the problem of prescription addiction is in our country. It is a deadly problem which has grown exponentially since my story aired across the country. Recently, the Health and Human Services Department determined that prescription addiction has become an epidemic in America. The American people make up about 5% of the world's population and yet we take approximately 80% of the world's narcotic prescriptions. Whole communities have been adversely affected when people become addicted to powerful narcotics drugs like OxyContin, Vicodin, Percodan, Norco, etc.

I was a wanderer with no permanent spiritual home. The brooms I'd captured while trying to change everything wrong in my life and this broken world were just another warped way of trying to *earn* love. I thought fighting all that was wrong in the world would prove me *worthy* of getting back home. The Bible reminds me, *"For it is by grace you have been saved, through faith--and this is not from yourselves, it is the gift of God." Ephesians 2:8.*

Sometimes we turn our blessings (our gifts from God) into *idols* and even after many years in recovery, my husband and I still relate to what we call the "grumbling Israelites" in the Old Testament of the Bible. They are the original "great forgetters" and I, too, have a "great forgetting" brain. God carried them out of bondage, indeed out of a lifetime of slavery in Egypt. He took care of their every need. Daily, they freely received manna from heaven and all they had to do was go out and collect it. God did not want them to save up or store it; He wanted them to trust in Him *everyday* for exactly what they needed. God was the originator of the "one day at a time" concept used in recovery.

Soon, however, those Israelites forgot all that God had done for them and began to grumble about not having meat and other things that they'd had back in Egypt. They even suggested that perhaps bondage was better. Isn't this still our human struggle today? We go from thinking about what amazing grace we have received to saying, "what's in it for me?" We can go from "thank you" to "poor me" in a matter of minutes. Next thing you know, we're having a pity party saying, "poor me, poor me, (and finally) pour me a drink!"

My life seems like it is a constant cycle in which my blessings become my burdens and my burdens become my blessings again. One day I find that I'm asking God for work, and then next day I'm complaining about having too much work. I will complain that my home is too small, and then move into a bigger one only to later complain that there is too much to clean. One day I'm complaining about the kids being too loud and messy and the next day they're gone and I'm complaining that I miss the noise and even the mess.

As we grow with God and learn from the painful experiences in our lives, we begin to see the blessings in those burdens. Then, just as suddenly, we begin to feel proud and start forgetting how we ended up here in the first place. Human beings, are *all* "great forgetters." I can go from grateful to grumbling in an instant. Even after God has turned a burden into a blessing for me, many times I turn around and make that blessing a burden once again.

For my 41st birthday my husband bought me a brand new Porsche. I love that car. It has a huge panoramic sunroof that covers the entire top of the car. My Porsche can switch from automatic to manual transmission with a touch of a button and it can go *way faster* than a mom like me would ever want to go. It is a very cool car and I love my husband for buying me such a fabulous birthday gift. Sometimes, however, I secretly long for the simplicity of my first car, Henry Honda. Henry Honda was a Honda Civic that could run forever on just one tank of gas. Henry Honda didn't need special gas or high performance, fancy tires. It didn't have a panoramic sunroof and could only drive in one transmission, but still, it was a great car. Johnny Z could do most of the maintenance on that car himself. When the time came to take Patsy Porsche into the dealer for a $1,000.00 oil and fluid change, I was *really* longing for the days of Henry Honda. But, Patsy Porsche and Henry Honda are both just cars. They are both little "h" happiness and will never be Big "H" Happiness no matter how fancy Patsy is or frugal Henry is. No matter how much money they cost or how much money they save, they will never be Big "H" Happiness; it's not in their DNA.

Having forgotten all of God's promises and His unchanging love, I was lost in this strange, far away land with no heart, no brain, and no courage. I understood those deeply rooted human feelings of inadequacy held by the three fictional friends from Oz. Never feeling good enough, smart enough, or brave enough to be successful in life or make a difference in the world. They knew they didn't have what it takes and I was right there with them.

"The Wizard of Oz" is a story which demonstrates our human failings and our search for wholeness through what John Calvin reminds us boils down to *tyranny,* I'm running the show, or *idolatry,* maybe this captured broom, rather than God, will fix me. I wish the Tin Man and I had known about the promise of Ezekiel 36:26-27, "*I will give you a new heart and put a new spirit in you; I will remove from you your heart of stone and give you a heart of flesh. And I will put my Spirit in you and move you to follow my decrees and be careful to keep my laws."* Tin Man and I had to learn the hard way that no human wizard can do it for us. You see, the human heart can only be satisfied by the One who made it. Only God could replace our hearts of stone.

Chapter Seven

Oz is a Big, Fat Phony

Searching for solutions offered by the world was exactly how I lived my life to this point. If society said something would make me happy and solve my problems, I was running for that solution. Dorothy and I trusted what the world told us to be true. We even sang as we went along, "We're off to see the Wizard, the wonderful Wizard of Oz."

When comparing the world's solutions to God's plan for our lives there are some obvious and distinct differences. After Dorothy captured the witch's broom, she and her friends rushed back to Oz, hopeful to finally receive the gifts which were *due* them. What happened next? He got angry and yelled at them. Even after they had done everything he had asked of them to do, precisely as he had asked it to be done, his fiery image projected on a screen yelled, "I can't believe my eyes! Why have you come back?" No one was joyful or celebrating success. Dorothy and her friends were shocked and bewildered. Oz thought he had given them an impossible task that they could *never* actually accomplish. He was setting them up to fail. He would never have to actually *help* them. He wasn't concerned about the well-being of Dorothy and her friends. He knew he was putting them in harm's way. So it is in our world.

The world sells ideas like; no matter the cost, we must be thin, rich, and famous. While the world would have us seeking solutions that often put us in harm's way, God *never* does. The world seeks perfection from us, all but ensuring that we will fail, but God *never* does. Society says that you will have finally *arrived* if you look good, have lots of money, and have great success. It doesn't care about how you got there or what it cost you. The world says you must earn *everything*, but God says we don't have to earn His love. We already have it.

When Toto pulled back the curtain, the group finally realized the shocking truth. Oz was just some old man from Kansas hiding behind a shower curtain and playing the big shot. A great sadness set in for each of them as they began to understand they would never realize their dreams. They had been chasing and believing a *lie*.

"The Great and Powerful Wizard of Oz" turned out to be just a big, fat phony. It was like all of my other worldly ideas which promised everything and delivered nothing. I spent my entire life to this point, looking for human solutions to a *spiritual* problem. I had forgotten a favorite verse from Romans 12:2 *"Do not conform to the pattern of this world, but be transformed by the renewing of your mind. Then you will be able to test and approve what God's will is—His good, pleasing and perfect will."*

I had been capturing broom after broom not for God, but for the world. Behind every great and powerful Oz there was just another human idea disguised as the "answer god." The problem was, those perfect human ideas were just that, human ideas. They were *idols* with maybe a touch of *tyranny*, too. If my perfect plans were enough to save me, well then, I wouldn't even *need* God. Oz, or in my case, the world, could have taken me home.

My recovery friends around the Emerald City kept reminding me that *lack of power* was my dilemma. Looking for the world to have the *real* power I needed was *the reason* I had a chronic relapse problem. At some point I had accepted the idea that I had an addiction, but I wasn't "all in" for their spiritual solutions. Stopping wasn't my problem. My problem was that *I couldn't stop starting again.* I was hopeless, so I used prescriptions, and I used prescriptions because I was hopeless. The years 1990-2003 were a constant cycle of relapse, recovery, and relapse again. I was like a hamster stuck on a treadmill with no way of getting off. I had a desire to stop my addiction, but I was nowhere near the *surrender* required in the First Step. When they said to attend as many meetings as possible, I attended a few. When they said work the steps like your life depends on it, I took it as just another box to check off, like getting to the gym or the grocery store.

We've heard it said that the definition of insanity is doing the same thing over and over again, expecting different results. I lived that definition for many years trying to solve my problem of prescription addiction with every solution offered by the world. Every time I try to run my life and power it all by myself, slowly, but surely, it begins to run me.

In the end, and only after being discovered in his lie, Oz the man, stepped out from behind the curtain and tried to make amends to the group by offering them trinkets. A diploma for Scarecrow to prove he was smart enough, a medal heart-shaped clock for Tin man, to prove he had a heart, and a medal of bravery for Lion, to prove he had courage.

How many times in my life did I seek those trinkets from the world expecting them to *change* me? The law that hangs in my office is one of those many trinkets. Awards, trophies, degrees, honors are nice and they help us remember the accomplishments in our lives, but they will *never* take us to where we are trying to go. They will never *transform* me or take me home.

When Oz, the man, finished handing out his trinkets, Dorothy was thrilled for Scarecrow, Lion and Tin man. Her friends suddenly realize that Dorothy didn't get anything for herself and they ask, "Hey, what about Dorothy?" Oz, the man, announced his plans to take Dorothy home to Kansas himself. In his giant hot air balloon he would carry them "home" to Kansas. Everyone was once again hopeful. Even after Dorothy realized that Oz was just a man and as human as she, Dorothy still believed maybe *he* could *save* her. She thought, maybe he really could take her back home in his hot air balloon. Again and again, I sought human solutions, such as Oz offers Dorothy, for my spiritual problems. And every time I would be left wondering - why am I always disappointed? Why don't my solutions work? Why does everyone let me down?

I had been lost in a foreign world for quite some time. The Bible says, *"If you belonged to the world, it would love you as its own. As it is, you do not belong to the world, but I have chosen you out of the world."* John 15:19. At the end of my journey in this strange new world, I was left all alone on a hot air balloon stand, watching Oz drift slowly away. All of my human solutions had failed me. While standing there I remembered something else my recovery friends from the Emerald City had told me, "When you're down to nothing, God is up to something."

Part Three: Recovery - God's Way

Chapter Eight

What a Gift, those Ruby Shoes

In our home, a butterfly picture hangs on the wall. Inside the butterfly are the words, "What the caterpillar calls the end of the world, the Master calls a butterfly." It is a hand-painted picture, nothing fancy, but I loved it from the first moment I saw it. That little butterfly picture, very simply, reminds me how many times in our lives, we think we are at the end of something. We think it's over for us. I'm sure that's what the caterpillar was thinking while he lay wrapped up tight in his mummy cocoon. Even in sadness and grief, the dying caterpillar was at the *beginning* of something much more wonderful than he could ever have imagined. I understand those feelings of impending doom that every caterpillar must surely experience. The world is coming to an end, something really bad is happening.

The end of the world came for me on October 16th, 2003

in the ICU at Mercy Folsom Hospital. Only a few weeks into my final relapse on prescription drugs, my grace had finally run out. From that hospital bed I knew I was dying. I knew my life was over. With my caterpillar eyes, I couldn't possibly see what the Master was doing. I could never have imagined what would happen.

They say that every addicted person has to hit his or her own bottom in their battle with addiction. My battle ended in all out war. I will jump to the very end in my fight to survive. My *ultimate surrender* came suddenly one October day. I was in the hospital once again for some very bad headaches and in no time at all, I was taking massive amounts of narcotics.

Once I would start on the narcotics it was like opening the floodgates. There are no words to truly describe the addiction. The closest I've found is to say that if you are addicted to opiates, you *need* them with every fiber of your being. Once I started taking opiates again, even if it had been quite some time in between, it was is if I had never stopped taking them. In fact, the addiction was even worse than before. After every relapse, it was more difficult to get off the prescriptions and living a sober life seemed more futile than ever before.

After years of relapses, I had built up quite a tolerance to prescription medications. In the hospital, I needed more with each passing hour. The doctors and nurses were amazed at how much medicine I could take. They had never seen anything like the tolerance I had for prescriptions and particularly narcotic opiate medications. I could take 100 milligrams of Demerol every 1-2 hours and that's just one of the many narcotics I was taking. To put that in perspective, one medical professional told me that a lethal dose of Demerol is about 1000 milligrams, yet I was taking that amount every 10-12 hours.

My family had spent the previous two weeks screaming at doctors and the hospital staff to stop the pain medications. They were telling them that I was a *prescription addict* and I should *never* be taking those drugs. Ultimately, I was in charge and the doctors were in this cycle with me, trying to figure out how to help. The doctors were in a quandary. What should they do with me? How could they help me as I screamed about the pain and demanded more and more of the pain medication that was *killing* me?

The simple fact was I had to help myself. I had to surrender and no one, no matter how smart, how well intentioned, or how much they loved me could surrender *for* me. I had accepted the fact that I was an alcoholic, but I still felt I was different than other alcoholics. I had seen so many people die of alcoholism and drug addiction. I had gone to so many funerals, but still I thought these things couldn't happen to *me*. I could never actually *die* from this addiction. Until, one day, I could.

After several days of huge amounts of round-the-clock intravenous opiates, I developed pneumonia in both lungs. Opiates slow down the respiratory system and after days of shallow breathing, my lungs had filled with fluid.

That October day, my body had had enough. As my lungs filled with fluid, I began to die. I knew I was dying and I knew *at that very moment* that *everything* my recovery friends said about my addiction was absolutely true. I was going to be another sad statistic and another unavoidable funeral for my family and friends to attend. I knew that afternoon what my funeral would look like. I knew how hard this would be on my loved ones. I knew the void this would leave in their lives and sadly, as I lay there dying, I knew with certainty that I had *chosen* for it to be this way.

As my lungs filled with fluid, my saturation rate dropped to around 50% and my breathing changed to what they call a death rattle. As I lay there, I heard the doctors and nurses running and yelling from my room and down the hall. My body felt like it was made of stone. I could not move any part of my body, not even my fingers or toes. My body was very stiff. It was exactly like I was an ice cold, stone figure lying there in that hospital bed. If you've ever been to an open casket funeral and touched the body of the dead person, that is exactly what I felt like, cold and rock hard, as if the spirit was already gone. There was no doubt in my mind what was happening to me at that point.

The moment that I lost all hope was the same moment that I began to pray. I prayed that day like I had never prayed before. I was no longer looking to Oz or a doctor to save me. I was no longer running the show. I was humbled before God and I began to beg Jesus to let me live. I begged Him to give me another chance. I would never turn to anything but Him again. Ever. I surrendered all. I kept praying, "Please let me live, Jesus, please help me, please, please, please."

At the foot of my bed was a very faint vision of my youngest daughter, Katie. She was only four years old at the time. She was just looking at me and I was begging God to let me stay with her and her big sister, Sarah, and my wonderful husband, John. I loved my family. I told God how much I loved them all and that they *needed* me. I said to Jesus, "Please let me stay; I will never, ever do this again". But, God in His infinite wisdom, let me struggle in that state of surrender, pleading for quite some time. For at least an hour I begged, I prayed, and I pleaded with my Maker for my life.

After a long time, I finally began to feel tingling in my fingers and I knew that God would let me have another chance at life. As my body became real again, I felt intense pain like someone was hitting me with a hammer. My prayer immediately changed to, "Thank you, God." I must have offered thanks to Jesus a million times from my bed in the ICU. Through tears of joy and thanksgiving, I was humbled before my Creator. Having clarity of mind, body, and sprit unlike anything I'd ever known, I knew that I was important to God that day and that He loved me *no matter what.*

Over the next few hours, the nurses would walk in with a syringe and I would yell, "No! Don't give me anything!" They were shocked. Was this not the same woman who was pushing the nurse's call button demanding drugs all day and all night? Something in me had profoundly changed. I didn't do it. God did it. I had asked and He had answered my prayer. I had been given the most precious gift of my life, the gift of mercy. The promise I made to God that day was a promise I intended to keep. I knew for certain that my grace had run out and that I was only alive because of His decision to extend me just a little more time on earth.

In the most sacred hour of my life I did not feel judgment from God, maybe sadness, but definitely not judgment. I certainly felt His love for me in a way I cannot fully describe. I will never question His love for me again. Since that day I've known with *certainty* how much God loves me and how much He loves every one of us. It is a perfect love He has for all of us in our broken, imperfect, and human conditions. I am eternally grateful for that love.

Before the day I lay dying in that hospital bed, I might have had lingering questions about my faith. Questions like: Who is God? And does He really care about me? Will I ever be good enough to be loved by God? That day in the hospital has increased my faith a thousand times. Since that frightening experience, I have been graced with a certainty about my faith which I cannot fully explain. I will never have those questions again. Today, when I pray, I know *exactly* who my Higher Power is. When you are all alone with your Creator, you know exactly whom you are addressing. It was **Jesus** I cried out to. And, it was **Jesus** who saved me. It was not some anonymous higher being, it was **Jesus** who brought me back to life and saved me from certain death.

The day He rescued me I was at the very *lowest* point of my life. I was in the most selfish, sinful, self-serving place I had ever been the day He reached down and saved me. All I had been thinking about was me, my needs, my desires, and my problems. I had certainly not proven myself worthy of any consideration from God. I had done *everything* wrong those weeks and months before that day at the hospital. Yet, He loved me and saved me!

So I surrendered all that day. My recovery friends had been saying for years that a spiritual awakening was required, but I never really understood what they were talking about. My husband, John, is such a blessing in my life and we have a truly beautiful life together today. But, at that point in our marriage, we had been really struggling mostly because of my prescription addiction. I may never fully understand the damage I caused throughout my prescription addiction. My addiction roared through the lives of my family and tore everything and everyone apart. With God's help, through it all we have grown stronger in our faith and in our love for Him and each other. It was as if

King David himself knew me and everyone lost in addiction, when he wrote Psalm 25:16-18, *"Turn to me and be gracious to me, for I am lonely and afflicted. The troubles of my heart are enlarged; bring me out of my distresses. Consider my affliction and my trouble, and forgive all my sins."* With that surrender prayer and many others like it, I began to get better.

Thankfully, John had recovery friends through the years to help him with his own feelings of being completely powerless to help his dying wife. He was with me one night in the ICU, as I told him the story about my end of life experience. I remember how scared and helpless he looked. When I finished telling him about my complete surrender to Jesus, he looked at me, wiping tears from his eyes, and he asked me, "Do you have your white flag?" I looked at my hospital wristband. It had been white, but now was covered with blood from the IV's. I looked at it and said, "I'll use this as my white flag." After a few silent moments he finally said, "Well, you'd better fly that mother-&%^#*!" (OK, I won't tell you *exactly* what he said☺)

Today, I keep that wristband, my white flag, in a clear plastic baggie. I bring it to meetings and I often talk with others about "my white flag" of surrender. My sponsor, Robin, made me another big white flag with the words, "Surrender" written across it. My white flag is a constant physical reminder of my final and complete surrender to God.

A few days after being released from the hospital, I had

a stroke. My left arm went numb and then completely limp and lifeless. Within seconds my face began to tingle and then went numb as well. My tongue felt huge and my speech began to be slurred. I could not move my face to smile or even to speak correctly. The MRI showed a small, but very important part of the brain had been affected with a small bleed. Initially, I had some paralysis on my upper left side, my arm, face and speech were affected. Within a few hours my speech came back, I was able to move my arm, and my face looked normal again. The numbness in my left hand became simple weakness and, for a few months, I could not hold anything heavy in my left hand.

Ultimately, it was determined that the stroke was a result of a blood clot from acute pneumonia caused by all the drugs. To this day, I still cannot type as fast with the left hand. My right hand often over types my left hand. My husband assures me that I will never make a living as a typist or a pianist anyway. But, my slow and weak left hand is a constant, physical reminder of my complete surrender to Jesus on that October day. I know this sounds strange, but I often find myself laughing as one hand types over the other and I always stop for a moment and thank God for this blessed reminder. I am alive. I am breathing in and out. I have another chance at life. "Thank you God!"

The weakness in my left hand is *my* "thorn in the flesh" just as Paul wrote about his "thorn in the flesh" in 2 Corinthians 12:7-10 *"Therefore, in order to keep me from becoming conceited, I was given a thorn in my flesh, a messenger of Satan, to torment me. Three times I pleaded with the Lord to take it away from me. But he said to me, "My grace is sufficient for you, for my power is made perfect in weakness." Therefore I will boast all the more gladly about my weaknesses, so that Christ's power may rest on me. That is why, for Christ's sake, I delight in weaknesses, in insults, in hardships, in persecutions, in difficulties. For when I am weak, then I am strong."*

My husband reminds me that God either "is" or He "isn't," there is no middle ground. *He is either everything or He is nothing at all.* Until the day in the hospital bed when I raised my white flag, I had been living as if the latter were true.

Like Dorothy, I later realized that someone had already given me the most precious gift of my life. My sparkling red ruby shoes symbolized my being washed in the blood of Jesus. That's all it takes. How had I forgotten His precious gift to me? So when I see red ruby shoes, it is with a grateful heart that I let these words wash over me. *"For I am convinced that neither death nor life, neither angels nor demons, neither the present nor the future, nor any powers, neither height nor depth, nor anything else in all creation, will be able to separate us from the love of God that is in Christ Jesus our Lord."* Romans 8: 38-39

When Glinda placed the ruby shoes on Dorothy's feet, Dorothy said, "They must be very powerful." Glinda reminded her that she must never take them off or she would be at the mercy of the wicked witch. For so many years, I put aside my faith. As Dorothy journeyed through the Land of Oz, she never realized the power of the ruby shoes, or the gift she'd been freely given. When I came to know Christ, I certainly didn't realize the power that was freely given to me. Like Dorothy, I was running around chasing brooms for men like Oz. I had no idea how to access the power. Long ago, Jesus had given me a gift of hope, a gift of love, a gift of grace, and it ensured my future. Those ruby shoes, which I had been wearing all along, were a life-saving gift that gave me a way back home.

I began by sharing the saying, "What the caterpillar calls the end of the world the Master calls a butterfly." Everyday, I meet and work with women who are becoming butterflies, but they cannot see what the Master is doing with their caterpillar eyes. To them it is the end of the world. I know today that part of my purpose in life, and the very reason for writing this book, is to help them see beyond the hopelessness they perceive with their caterpillar eyes. Everyday, I get to help them see the hope that God has for their future. I'm so grateful for the recovery miracles that He is doing all around me. *"Therefore, if anyone is in Christ, he is a new creation; the old has gone, the new has come!" 2 Corinthians 5:17*

There is another saying which hangs in our Alano Club, "Those who see God's hand in everything, are better at leaving everything in God's hands." For the first time in my life, I was beginning to see God's hand in everything. So, for my final trip Home, I've decided to let Him carry me in His mighty and merciful hands. That way I know, I'll never be lost again.

Chapter Nine

Accepting God's Love - It's an Inside Job

While Dorothy's journey was fictional, mine was very real. Glinda's gift to Dorothy was her ruby shoes. God's gift to me (and all of us) is Jesus.

The shoes had the power to transport Dorothy back home. She simply needed to surrender by clicking her heels three times, (waving her white flag) and saying, "There's no place like home, there's no place like home, there's no place like home." I understood Dorothy when she said, "But, it is so simple, I should have figured it out long ago." When her friends said, "We should have done it for her." Glinda offers, *"She had to figure it out for herself."*

All I had to do was simply accept this precious Gift from God. I needed to raise my white flag of surrender from my will to God's will. I began in earnest this time, down the yellow brick road, not towards the Emerald City in search of Oz, but to a far better place. I was finally heading Home.

Many months after my story aired on the CBS Evening News, an Executive News Producer called to ask a question. She wanted to know what it meant when someone would say, "I'm a friend of Bill W." Over the years she had seen a News Executive who refused to accept calls from Ambassadors or Senators or other important people, but she said, if someone called the newsroom and simply said, "I need to talk with him, I'm a friend of Bill W.," he would *always* drop everything and take the call. I didn't have to answer her question. She was a smart woman and she understood what it meant. It was further confirmation of my faith in a recovery community who tries to be there for each other.

I often think of a busy News Executive putting the "important people" on hold while taking the call from an unimportant (at least by the world's standards) friend in need. Maybe he *knew* there was something bigger going on than what the world keeps telling us. Perhaps that busy News Executive had heard the story of the lost coin from Luke 15. *"In the same way, I tell you, there is rejoicing in the presence of the angels of God over one sinner who repents." Luke 15:10* Clearly, he understood the *real* importance of helping that one lost friend find his way home.

At one of the world conventions, during the end of the meeting one night, John recorded the sound of the Lord's

Prayer on his phone being said by 70,000 alcoholics. Many times over the years, we've listened to those 70,000 once lost souls saying that prayer. Sometimes, I think I can actually hear the heavens rejoicing as they pray. It reminds me of the story of the prodigal son. One son stays home and does everything right while the other goes out and does everything wrong. Why would God care so much when the lost son returns home? Why did He love me so much when I was so lost? Only through the perspective of a parent do those passages begin to make sense. There is nothing my girls could ever do to make me love them more than I already do. Likewise, there is nothing they could ever do to make me love them any less. That doesn't mean that I always agree with them, but they've never had to *earn* my love, they simply *have* it.

As a Law Enforcement Chaplain, unfortunately, we see many suicide cases. I once heard a father of a child who had committed suicide give some advice for parents. He said to remind your children that there is no problem too great that God cannot help you solve and that there is no sin so big that God cannot forgive. He loves us no matter what, just as we love our children, *no matter what*. To overcome a huge problem like prescription drug addiction, I needed to *know* this kind of love and I had to figure it out for myself.

Often in the evenings after supper, my husband and I go for walks with our girls. There is so much we hear about their days at the dinner table or on those walks. One night, our oldest daughter, Sarah was talking about a pre-calculus/trigonometry class she had just started her junior year of high school. She was feeling "less than" and really intimidated by the class. She said all the students in the class were smarter than her and most had come from foreign countries. They had different faiths and cultures. She wondered if she should just drop the class. Sarah had already fulfilled her math requirements to graduate high school, so why was she taking this class anyway? But, deep down, she knew why. You see, Sarah loves math and she really wanted to take the class. She just didn't have the confidence she needed.

After hearing Sarah out, John and I told her that perhaps she was exactly right. The kids in that class *were* different from her in many ways. We told her that most of them probably *were* a lot smarter than she was. But, we encouraged her not to assume things about others. We reminded her that she didn't actually *know* how they felt about her. She was just guessing. "Besides," we said, "what other people think about you is not your business, it's God's business." We suggested that she focus on trying to *be* a good friend to others in that class and worry less about *having* friends. Finally, we told her to study hard and give it her all, leaving the outcomes in God's hands.

At the end of that school year, on another walk, Sarah was going on and on about all the new friends she had made that year. Those kids, whom she had been so afraid of at the beginning of the year, had become some of her *closest* friends. We laughed about how our first impression of others is often just flat out wrong. I suggested to Sarah that she make a permanent memory of all those feelings of inadequacy, which she had felt, at the beginning of that class. We encouraged her to remember how it had turned out to be just a false fear. Another acronym for F.E.A.R. is False Evidence Appearing Real. The quantitative mind of the math student in her would never forget this important life lesson. Throughout our lifetimes, the devil often takes a run at us by telling us we are less than others (just like the Tin Man, Scarecrow, and Lion felt they weren't good enough, smart enough, or brave enough).

12-Step recovery has taught me a great deal about myself. John and I are passing along those recovery tools to our girls in hopes of breaking a cycle of addiction which often affects families for generations. Understanding our nature is an important part of our recovery journey. Sarah knows today that while she may not be the smartest kid in the class, if she works hard, she can still do well and contribute something in every situation. After graduation she was a finalist in a medical scholarship from a local hospital. The interview panel explained that they loved the honesty in her essay about her struggles with a learning disability, but suggested when she wrote, *"Most of my friends today are smarter than I am, but we help each other. Many of my friends are from other countries, and I've been able to help them meet new people and feel more at home in America,"* they begged to differ. Having Sarah's academic credentials before them, they said to her, "Sarah, the other students are not smarter than you." She thought for a moment, then smiled and said, "Well, you don't know my friends. They really *are* smarter than me." Everyone burst into laughter and she won the medical scholarship award. My point is this; we need to be *authentic*, even if the honest answer might not always look good.

Those feelings of inadequacy follow us all the time, even when we're older and should know better. I wish my friend Maryanne, who died long ago, had stuck around recovery to learn this with me. I think of the time when I ran my first 10K race. I'd been training really hard for several months and I sensed I was ready. The morning of the race I was so excited and I felt really official as pinned on my numbered bib and timing chip. John dropped me off at the starting line. He and the girls were going to meet me at the finish line. Before he left, I looked around at all the other 10K runners. They looked like professional runners and I was suddenly paralyzed with fear. Who was I kidding? I said to John, "I can't do this. These are *real* runners. I'm not a real runner." He smiled, put his hand on my head and said a sweet prayer for me. When he finished his prayer, he lifted his head and he looked me right in the eyes. He said, "Now, go have FUN!" I finished that race, not at the top, but not even close to the bottom either. Here's the important part, I had FUN running it and I finished it even though I was afraid.

I used to have a cartoon which hung on my refrigerator with a little boy saying to his friend, "I think my brain is trying to kill me." I know that my best thinking is usually wrong and that I can't fix my broken brain with my broken brain. I've also heard it said that my mind is like a bad neighborhood and I should never go there alone. Recovery is a "we" solution. God's solutions always come in the "we," not the "me."

A few years ago, our family went to the Grand Canyon. On our last night, NASA was doing a Star Gazing seminar and we had the opportunity to see millions of stars and planets up close. Through those huge NASA telescopes we could see as far as four galaxies away. Some of those galaxies were 50 million light years from earth. It was an incredible night under the stars with the stars of my life here on earth. I'll never forget that night in the Grand Canyon with John, Sarah, and Katie. We thanked God that evening for so many blessings in our lives, especially for being able to see His glorious creation and sharing it together.

The very next night we were in Las Vegas. While walking down the Las Vegas strip enjoying the flashing lights from the casinos, we looked up to point out the stars we had seen from the night before. Although it was a clear night, they were nowhere to be found. They were up there for sure, but because of the bright lights from this big city, our view of them was completely blocked. While the lights of Las Vegas were appealing, our family knew that night they were nothing compared to what God was doing in the skies above. The hidden stars made us sad.

Walking back, we talked about how many times in our lives we build grand things, maybe even distractions, which only serve to block us from God. Those Las Vegas lights were just more captured brooms trying to show off worldly accomplishments. Maybe some are even trying to outshine God. Remember the original sin in the Garden of Eden when the serpent suggests to Eve you can be *like* God? My recovery friends know that the devil uses pride to trip us up *all* the time. That night in Las Vegas we knew that nothing we could ever build or do in life would *ever* "out fancy" God. Why would we even try?

At the end of many 12-Step meetings, we make a circle, hold hands, and say the Lord's Prayer together. Then, we often say, "Keep coming back. It works if you work it." Usually we add, "And work it, 'cause you're worth it!" You see, we all have setbacks and failures in life, but we don't have to let the evil one make us feel defeated after each knockdown. The devil loves to tell us that that extra ten pounds we gained, the money we lost because of our bad choices, or even our selfish behavior, is *proof* that we will never be good enough. Failure prompts feelings of inadequacy in all of us and the devil ceases those moments of insecurity. That's when we need to remember that God is already there. He loves us *unconditionally.* All we need to do is trust Him. Our broken, but faithful friends, will help us remember to "Keep coming back" to Him. That saying, "It works, if you work it and work it 'cause you're worth it!" reminds me of 1 Thessalonians 5:11 *"Therefore encourage one another and build one another up, just as you are doing."* Mostly that means helping each other *remember* how much God loves us.

For Dorothy and her wonderfully broken friends, Scarecrow, Tin Man, and Lion, their feelings of inadequacy were feelings that everyone understands. But, if we open our mouths and talk about it with our other broken friends, they can often help us see the path ahead. Sometimes we are just too scared. Sometimes we are standing at the starting line with our number and timing chip on, all ready to go, and then in an instant we're overcome with fear. We want to give up. We cannot see the finish line all by ourselves. Hopeless and helpless is how we all *start* to get better. When we are finally sick and tired of being sick and tired, we gather our broken friends, lock arms and start singing and dancing our way down the yellow brick road. And we continue to sing and dance, even if our voices are shaking as we sing and our legs are wobbling as we dance along.

Chapter Ten

Steps Toward Home

When I was a little girl, my grandfather owned a small grocery store in downtown Lubbock, Texas. I used to love to go to work with Granddad and spend the day playing in his store. It seemed to me that Granddad knew everyone in Lubbock, Texas. All day long he'd visit with people and help them with their grocery needs. I remember around the noontime hour, he would go to the back room and start cutting big hunks of cheese and sometimes, if it had been a good day for sales, he'd slice up some bologna. I'd sit and peel off the red strings as Granddad started to make sandwiches for the local drunks who were hanging around downtown. It wasn't a government program or organized in any way. Granddad just saw a need and he filled it.

Many of those alcoholics would take the sandwich with dirty, shaky hands, but with gratitude in their eyes. We knew this was perhaps the only food they would consume that day. Even at a young age, as I watched them eat, I knew my grandfather was making a good difference. He loved those hopeless alcoholics in his own special way. I never heard him speak badly about them. He just served them and let God handle the rest.

Several years later, when I arrived at a doctor's office shaky and hopeless from prescription addiction, it was the doctor's wife who took me into their small office break room, sat me down and do you know what she did? She made me a cheese sandwich. As I sat there, broken and crying, she told me not to try to figure my life out, but to simply listen and start following some simple instructions. Sometimes love comes in the form of a simple cheese sandwich. I've seen that love demonstrated throughout my lifetime. I've felt that kind of love and today I get to share it with others who need to feel it, too.

While the munchkins sing, "follow the yellow brick road," my recovery friends say, at every meeting, "Rarely have we seen a person fail who has *thoroughly* followed our path." Bill Wilson, one of the founders of Alcoholics Anonymous, was once asked if there was anything he would change about the Big Book of Alcoholics Anonymous. He said he would change only one word. He would change the word "rarely" and replace it with the word, "never." So it would read, "*Never* have we seen a person fail who has *thoroughly* followed our path." Needless to say, those recovery friends are pretty sure about their path. Their path is 12 simple, but not easy, steps.

Recovery through the 12-Steps can be found in a variety of ways. There are numerous meetings and groups which offer 12-Step solutions. There is surely a 12-Step group for any of life's problems. Many churches now offer 12-Step Bible studies and workshops. Many community centers, Alano clubs, church buildings, libraries, etc. offer a variety of 12-Step programs.

Bill Wilson and Dr. Bob were co-founders of Alcoholic's Anonymous from which the 12-Steps originated. The religious training of these two great men began in Christian churches and from biblical teachings. Bill Wilson had been a member of the Oxford Group, which was a Christian fellowship, and the 12-Steps were an expansion of the Oxford Six Steps. So, while the 12-Steps came from Bible life application principles, they were written in a very *general* way in hopes of being *inclusive* of everyone from *all* faiths and for those who have no faith at all. No matter what a person's religious faith, his or her theological training, or lack thereof, the 12-Step process can work for anyone. Bill Wilson knew that God would meet them right where they were. Anyone who has a *surrender* problem, or a *sin* problem of *any* kind, and has a sincere desire to change his or her life can benefit from the practice of the 12-Steps.

So, I ran back to meetings and got back on the path which they had laid out before me. In a very real sense, God brought me to 12-Step recovery and 12-Step recovery brought me *all* the way back to God. In one of the first meetings I went back to after getting out of the hospital, I found a sponsor to help me along that path and re-worked the 12-Steps with her. I had always had good sponsorship, but you know how they say, when the student is ready the teacher appears? Well, Ann H. appeared at one of my first meetings after I crawled out of the hospital. She was dragging her oxygen tank up to the podium to speak and she went on to talk about the importance of showing up and being of service. She was such a funny lady with a great since of humor. She said things like, "Meeting makers make it" and "Change, we must, or drink we will." We like to think of those sayings as "Ann-isms." She always made perfect sense to me and her attitude matched my newfound optimism. As far as I know, Ann coined the phrase, "Once you're a pickle, you'll never be a cucumber again." Ann knew me well, even before I knew myself. She made it seem simple for me. She took me back through the steps and I cannot begin to explain the difference she and those spiritual steps made in my life.

For the first time in a long time, I was getting right with God and with the world around me. God was in charge of my life; He was my Power. Suddenly, I understood the scripture, *"A man's steps are directed by the Lord. How then can anyone understand his own way?" Proverbs 20:24*

12-Steps worked like this for me: Steps 1, 2, and 3 were

about surrender and getting right with God. I call the first three steps my "Salvation Steps." Steps 4-9 are about getting right with the world around me. I call these steps my "Sanctification Steps." Steps 10, 11, and 12 are about *staying* right with God and the world around me, I call them my "Serenity Steps." Rick Warren, author of "The Purpose Driven Life" says that we were designed by God and for His good purposes. Until we understand that fact, our lives will never make sense. The practice of 12-Step and biblical application recovery helped me begin to make sense of my life.

Many years before, I had been in a Big Book study probably critiquing their book and sitting in judgment of the recovery programs, but I heard the leader of the study say something that caught my attention. It was about understanding our motives. He said that you can help clean up after the meeting because you want everyone to see you and say, "Wow, look at her helping so much." Or, you can help clean up after the meeting simply because it needs to be done. Then he said, "Only you and God know the difference." I realized that I never did anything just because it needed to be done. Everything I did seemed to have a selfish motive attached to it. Working the 12-Steps was one of the first honest things I did, just because it *needed* to be done.

Our path began on Step One. Ann and I would meet every Tuesday and work a step. There are a number of wonderful resources for going through the 12-Steps. Over the years I've used a variety of different tools in taking the steps, but I've come to know that most good ideas are simple. I thought I'd share a simple overview of the 12-Steps.

Step One is "We admitted we were powerless over alcohol and that our lives had become unmanageable." I've always loved the Apostle Paul from the Bible. In my mind, he was an original 12-Stepper. When I get to heaven, I'm going to find him right away. I love what Paul said in *Romans 7:18, "I know that nothing good lives in me, that is, in my sinful nature. For I have the desire to do what is good, but I cannot carry it out."* Paul had been a Christian for a very long time when he wrote those words and they are the essence of Step One. I am powerless over *sin* in my life. I need God's help to get better.

Jesus said in *Matthew 26:41, "The spirit is willing but the body is weak."* Being fully human and fully God, I wonder if Jesus wasn't demonstrating for us a human need for each of us to take Step One. Remarkably, He made this admission for us, right before His crucifixion. The next verse, Matthew 26:42, Jesus says, *"My Father, if it is not possible for this cup to be taken away unless I drink it, may your will be done."* In those two verses, in the Garden of Gethsemane, Jesus humbly demonstrates for us steps one, two, and three.

In today's world, saying I can't or I surrender sometimes seems like failure. By the world's standards it is not good to appear weak or admit failure. But in the Spiritual world, the exact opposite is true. Paul again writes in 2 Corinthians 12:10, *"For when I am weak, then I am strong."*

Step One begins with "We admitted we." This journey is such a "we" thing and the first thing you learn from the first word in the first step is exactly that point. We are completely powerless to live the life that God has called us to live all by ourselves. We *need* each other. I once heard a joke about a man who had fallen into a deep hole and couldn't get out. A priest walked by and the man yelled for help. The priest said I will pray for you and he walked on down the road. Next, an engineer walked by as the man yelled for help. The engineer drew up an elaborate escape route design on a piece of paper and tossed it down to the man in the hole. Finally, an alcoholic walked by and when the man screamed for help, the alcoholic jumped in the hole. The man said, "Are you crazy? Now we are both stuck in this hole." The alcoholic simply smiled and said, "No, we aren't. I have been stuck in this hole before and I know the way out!"

Finally, it is said that Step One is the only step we must do perfectly, with 100% surrender. My struggle for so many years centered on my inability to completely surrender. I think I had a desire to stop doing what I'd been doing, but that was nowhere near a full, and utter surrender required in Step One.

Step Two is "Came to believe that a power greater than

ourselves could restore us to sanity." Put simply, "I can't (Step One)," and "He can (Step Two)." I have always believed in God, but I have not always believed that this Omnipotent (all powerful), Omniscient (all knowing), Omnipresent (fully everywhere) God loved me completely and unconditionally, no matter what. That's the only kind of God I could really surrender to. As I mentioned in an earlier chapter, if I could do it by myself, I wouldn't need God. But, I do. I always have and I always will need God. I cannot even love others without God, who is in a very real sense, Love. *"Whoever does not love does not know God, because God is love." 1 John 4:8*

Step Three says, "Made a decision to turn our will and our lives over to the care of God as we understood Him." The first three steps are simply decision steps. I can't (Step One), He can (Step Two), I'll let Him (Step Three). The third step prayer is a great prayer which my husband and I pray everyday. We pray the third step prayer with our children, often on the way to school. This is the third step prayer:

"God, I offer myself to Thee--to build with me and to do with me as Thou wilt. Relieve me of the bondage of self, that I may better do Thy will. Take away my difficulties, that victory over them may bear witness to those I would help of Thy Power, Thy Love, and Thy Way of life. May I do Thy will always! Amen."

Sometimes we stop after the phrase, "bondage of self," and think about what that means at this moment in time. We often tease each other around our home by saying, I'm not much, but I'm all I think about. Unfortunately, that is true for most of us. Alcohol-ISM is often described with the acronym, "I.S.M." (I. Self. Me.) Bottom-line, it's not about me. *Romans 12:1 says, "Therefore, I urge you, brothers, in view of God's mercy, to offer your bodies as living sacrifices, holy and pleasing to God. This is your spiritual act of worship."* It's all about serving God and loving His kids, just as my grandfather did by making those simple cheese sandwiches everyday.

The next phrase from the third step prayer is, "take away my difficulties." I usually pause to reflect with my family and friends about what exactly my difficulties are just for today. Sometimes we list those things realizing that the rest of the prayer says, *"Take away my difficulties, that victory over them may bear witness to those I would help of Thy Power, Thy Love, and Thy Way of life. May I do Thy will always! Amen."* Just like Jesus right before His crucifixion, we end our prayer, the third step prayer, with "may I do Thy will always" or "Thy will be done."

Many people come into recovery and get stuck doing the 1, 2, 3 waltz. But, we are often reminded that these are decision steps. If a frog sits on a lily pad and decides to jump into the water, how do you know what he has decided to do? You know because the frog *jumps* from his lily pad into the water. So I jumped from the lily pad of steps one, two and three and into refreshing waters of steps four through twelve. But, the rest are *action steps* so I had to start swimming.

Step Four says, "Made a searching and fearless moral inventory of ourselves." Step Four is often one of the most feared steps, but it is one of the most powerful and life changing steps, as well. In the inventory steps, the real magic begins. Step Four is where we start to understand ourselves, perhaps for the very first time. It is where we learn to forgive and be forgiven and where we start to get better. Looking at my part in every situation is not easy, especially when someone has really hurt me. Ultimately, the only thing I can do anything about is me - my attitudes and my actions. That task alone is pretty big.

I've heard it said that if you don't take a fourth, you'll drink a fifth. So, I did an honest fourth step. The Bible says, *"Let us examine our ways and test them, and let us return to the Lord." Lamentations 3:40.* Step Four is our beginning. Johnny Z describes it as if we are carrying around a giant backpack full of heavy rocks all our lives and in Step Four we start pulling out the rocks and making peace with them. In the next step, we start laying them down at the cross.

Step Five is, "Admitted to God, to ourselves, and to another human being the exact nature of our wrongs." When I did this step with sweet Ann, I was ready to dump everything. All of my deepest and darkest secrets, I wanted and needed to let go. We are only as sick as our secrets and we all have them. I used to think that secrets were just things alcoholics carried around, but after a few years of working as a Law Enforcement Chaplain, I've realized that *everyone* has regrets and *everyone* has secrets. All of us have things which haunt us and keep us from God. Finishing Step Five was one of the most freeing experiences in my life. My load was so much lighter after taking Step Five. I felt the promise from Isaiah 44:22, *"I have swept away your offenses like a cloud, your sins like the morning mist. Return to me, for I have redeemed you."*

Why do we take Step Five with another human being? Why can't I just do this with God and me? There are many good reasons. Denial is such a big part of our problem, it is hard, if not impossible, to see ourselves clearly. Even after years of recovery, I still need others to help me see myself clearly. I think the best reason, however, is found in the book of James 5:16, *"Therefore confess your sins to each other and pray for each other so that you may be healed."* God knows how much we need each other. Remember, He *designed* us to need others.

Step Six is, "Were entirely ready to have God remove all these defects of character." After doing steps four and five, I started realizing that I was at fault in so many conflicts in my life. I really wanted to get better. I wanted to stop my old behavior and, for the first time in my life, I began to *believe* that I could. That hope was fulfilled in this scripture, *"Humble yourself before the Lord and He will lift you up."* James 4:10

There is another recovery promise which says, "We are

going to know a new freedom and a new happiness before we are halfway through." I was halfway through the steps, and I was already skipping along, singing and dancing, and feeling free.

The seven deadly sins were a good starting point to look at my character defects. The seven deadly sins are: pride, sloth, lust, greed, envy, anger, and gluttony. Perhaps the opposite of those sins are the fruits of the Spirit, from *Galatians 5:22-23, they are love, joy, peace, forbearance, kindness, goodness, faithfulness and self-control.* One list is a *burden* that comes when I focus on *self,* and the other list is a *blessing* which comes when I focus on *God and others.*

Step Seven is, "Humbly asked Him to remove our shortcomings." Six and seven are a daily practice in my life. The seventh step prayer is another prayer which I say everyday. Here is the seventh step prayer:

"My Creator, I am now willing that you would have all of me, good and bad. I pray that You remove from me every single defect of character which stands in the way of my usefulness to You and my fellows. Grant me strength as I go from here to do Your bidding. Amen."

I usually pause at the part of the prayer which says, "remove from me every single defect of character" and I talk with my Creator God about what those are today. Every day it is a bit different, but over time I have come to learn what motivates me to act the way I do. Through this process I have learned what causes me to be fearful, insecure, and what makes me happy. One step at a time, one day at a time, I've come a long way from the girl holding a "feelings chart" trying to identify a simple feeling.

My pastor, Dr. G. Henry Wells, said that a good definition of humility is walking in the shadow of God. I often imagine myself following Him around. I can always decide to step away from God and go it alone; it never works out well for me when I do.

In the Bible, there is a place referred to as the "threshing floor." It was a dirty, busy workplace. When they would harvest wheat, the threshing floor would become a messy place of activity. They would bring in the harvest and then begin the hard work of separating the good wheat from the bad. The 6th and 7th steps are about asking God to remove my character defects. Many of them are found on the threshing floor where the husks and the tares would lie after the good wheat was harvested. The removal of the good from the bad is an ongoing, lifelong process. Like laundry, it never ends.

I find it interesting that God chose the threshing floor, of all places, to have King David build an altar. To God, the threshing floor was much more than just a work area. The threshing floor was a place of importance. It was a workplace, a meeting place, and a place of worship and celebration. Throughout time, the threshing floor has been a holy and sacred place where hard work is done and where *real* worship begins.

I think maybe God loves the threshing floor for the same reasons that I've come to love those dreaded steps 4 through 10. Those are the steps where you really have to work hard and be willing to go to *any* length to get better. I think of them as my personal threshing floor. Today I know that those threshing floor steps prepare me for the altar of God.

C.S. Lewis said that the definition of humility is not thinking less of yourself, it is thinking of yourself less. The next two steps require a person with exactly that type of humility. Not someone with low self esteem, but someone who is humble, yet strong in their faith, and willing to follow God wherever He leads, even if it's into the hornet's nest to make amends to others.

Step Eight says, "Made a list of people we had harmed and became willing to make amends to them all." This is a simple list done with a sponsor. There are many wonderful things which God does when we set out to atone for our sins and make amends to those we've harmed. *2 Corinthians 5:19 says, "For God was reconciling the world to himself in Christ, not counting men's sins against them. And he has committed to us the message of reconciliation."* God in heaven is surely rejoicing as we make our eighth step list!

Step Nine; you guessed it, "Made direct amends to such people wherever possible, except when to do so would injure them or others." There are many miracles which I have seen when people seeking to live in God's will begin to practice steps eight and nine. An entire book could be written about the life changing experiences which are the fruits of practicing these "amends" steps. They are about reconciliation. Through these steps God begins to reconcile us to Him and to each other. We just do the footwork and trust in Him. He controls the outcomes.

Step Ten says, "Continued to take personal inventories and when we were wrong, promptly admitted it." Daily inventories have helped me to change my life one day at a time. Sometimes life feels overwhelming, but I can do anything just for today. This step helps to keep me focused on keeping it simple. Brick by brick, step by step, I keep heading towards Home.

Step Ten for me is done every night. Over the years, I've used all kinds of tools to help me with Step Ten. *2 Corinthians 13:5 says, "Examine yourselves to see whether you are in the faith; test yourselves."* So every night, I try to review my day. I ask God to help me see the good parts of my day, the things I need to be grateful for as well as all the areas of my day that I need to do better. Do I owe an amends to someone for my actions today? Over time, these personal inventories have helped me to know myself better and to really grow in my journey with Jesus. *"So if you think you are standing firm, be careful that you don't fall." 1 Corinthians 10:12* Step Ten also helps me to keep from filling up my backpack with rocks again.

There is a phrase in the Big Book which says, "Our primary purpose is to fit ourselves to be of maximum service to God and to the people about us." I remember thinking in early recovery, that that didn't sound like very much fun. I secretly worried that if I stuck around the Emerald City very long I might end up working at a soup kitchen behind the castle. None of my recovery friends were worried that God would sentence me to a life I hated. But, still I worried about it. How could a life, based on humble service to others, bring any real and lasting joy? When I'd share those fears with my new friends, they would laugh and say things like, we are sure that God wants us to be happy, joyous, and free. Or they would offer a phrase from the Big Book like, "We absolutely insist on being happy." But mostly, they just told me to get busy, make coffee, set up chairs, or call someone who needed help. They knew that I needed to stop trying to figure it all out. They knew that I couldn't *think* my way into right living, but that I could *act* my way into *right thinking*.

I know that real joy is found in loving and serving others, not in how much we are loved or served *by* them. *Mark 10:45 says, "For even the Son of Man did not come to be served, but to serve others."* Service to others always brings me back to the truth about what has happened in my life. My alcoholic amnesia is treated and reversed by staying close to recovery and continuing to put my hand out to help others. I've been given a daily reprieve, just like manna from heaven. I cannot store it up or live off yesterday's recovery. Everyday I must do the work and the 10th Step is part of my daily practice.

My recovery friends have taught me that that my daily reprieve is contingent upon the *maintenance* of my spiritual condition. My sponsor today, Robin D., reminds me that it does not say that I have a daily reprieve contingent on my *spiritual condition*, but on the *maintenance* of my spiritual condition. She says that I can always work on the maintenance of my spiritual condition, but that the spiritual condition itself (how I *feel* my life is going) is always in God's hands.

Step Eleven is, "Sought through prayer and meditation to improve our conscience contact with God, as we understood Him, praying only for knowledge of His will for us and the power to carry that out." A whole step is devoted to prayer and meditation. Why is prayer and meditation so important? It is through this process that we begin to tap into that Power which we all need so desperately. This is where we connect with God and learn to hear His guidance and discern His will for our lives.

I used to think I was pretty good at prayer, but terrible at meditation. Then I read something else Pastor Rick Warren said about meditation. He said, "If you can worry, you can meditate." He went on to say that worry is meditation. It's just meditation on self, rather than on God. I needed to really start surrendering to the awesome power and will of God through Step Eleven. I started refocusing my prayers and meditation.

Throughout the day, I often ask God to direct my thinking. *"We take captive every thought to make it obedient to Christ." 2 Corinthians 10:5* There are many other great prayers. The Lord's Prayer is a great prayer of submission and protection, which we all need everyday. It is a corporate prayer for the world around me and helps me to get out of myself and pray for others. The Lord's Prayer is the closing prayer in most 12-Step meetings.

There is another wonderful prayer that reminds us to focus on what we can bring to the world rather than what we can get from it. The prayer of Saint Francis is also called the 11th Step prayer and it is one of my very favorites.

The Prayer of St. Francis of Assisi
Lord, make me a channel of thy peace,
that where there is hatred, I may bring love,
that where there is wrong, I may bring the spirit of forgiveness,
that where there is discord, I may bring harmony,
that where there is error, I may bring truth,
that where there is doubt, I may bring faith,
that where there is despair, I may bring hope,
that where there are shadows, I may bring light,
that where there is sadness, I may bring joy.
Lord, grant that I may seek rather to comfort than to be comforted,
to understand, than to be understood,
to love, than to be loved.
For it is by self-forgetting that one finds. It is by forgiving that one is forgiven. It is by dying that one awakens to eternal life. Amen.

Step Twelve, is "Having had a Spiritual Awakening as a result of these steps, we tried to carry this message to alcoholics who still suffer, and to practice these principles in all our affairs." This whole step is devoted to loving and serving other people. Service work used to be just another obligation, but today, it has become a privilege and an honor to serve others.

Step Twelve blesses those who practice it. Sometimes when life gets tough and I simply don't have the answers I need, setting aside my little problems and reaching out in service to others will save the day. Every week I work with women who are just beginning their journey in taking the 12-Steps. They are scared and unsure, but I have hope for them just as so many others had hope enough for me when I began my journey. *"Praise be to the God and Father of our Lord Jesus Christ, the Father of compassion and the God of all comfort, who comforts us in all our troubles, so that we can comfort those in any trouble with the comfort we ourselves receive from God."* 2 Corinthians 1:3-4 Together, we will get Home.

Dr. Bob, right before his death in 1950, once said that it all boils down to love and service. I can tell you today that God has changed my heart and, like Dorothy in the last scene, I feel gratitude beyond measure. God is good and I have come to see His blessings in everything. Mother Teresa said, "Spread love everywhere you go: first of all in your own house. Give love to your children, to your wife or husband, to a next door neighbor. Let no one ever come to you without leaving better and happier. Be the living expression of God's kindness; kindness in your face, kindness in your eyes, kindness in your smile, kindness in your warm greeting."

I know today that service *begins* at home. God brought our family together to help one another. We are the VIPs in each other's lives. We always take each other's calls and spend quality time together learning and enjoying life. Our family is a blessing, a gift from God. Sunday dinners are a regular part of our extended family routine. Every Sunday after church, we gather everyone together. Grandparents, cousins, uncles and aunts, and sometimes even some stray friends, we hold hands, pray, and eat together. We are there for each other in *all* of life's situations, the blessings and the burdens. My family can spend hours, even days and weeks planning a prank, a skit, or some other "gotcha" to pull on each other. I can assure you that there is no way you could grow up in my family and not know how to laugh at yourself. They've taught me how to enjoy life and really live it once again. I am forever grateful that 12-Step recovery has helped me heal the family wounds I caused during my prescription addiction. Those 12-Steps are the foundation which God used to help rebuild my life.

Quiet service to others is a way of life for my 12-Stepping friends. I once heard a story about a flight attendant who was about sixty days sober and had just started back to work after coming out of rehab. At the end of a long flight into LAX, she suddenly had an overwhelming desire to drink. The thought consumed her. She really didn't want to drink. She knew she would lose her job and much more if she started drinking again. She knew that the compulsion was so great that she had no choice and eventually, that desire to drink would overcome her. Still, she really wanted to stay sober.

In a last ditch effort to stay sober that day, the flight attendant walked over to an empty gate and picked up a phone. She simply asked the operator to make an announcement to see if friends of Bill W. could please come to Gate 12. Within minutes, over the loud speaker the announcer repeated several times, "Will friends of Bill W. please come to Gate 12?" Almost immediately, people started showing up. Many came from all over the airport to help a fellow friend in need whom they had never met before. The flight attendant was moved to tears when she realized that some had missed their flights, even getting out of lines boarding airplanes to help an anonymous friend. When they heard the call for help, they automatically responded. Needless to say, the flight attendant, along with dozens of other sober friends, did not drink that day.

There are many stories like this one with my 12-Stepping friends. Service to others has become a way of life for those touched by the power of a merciful God. Just like me, they were once hopeless and lost, but they've learned to start 12-Stepping in their Ruby Shoes and get busy helping others. If you look around, you will find them doing 12-Step work everywhere. You will notice them right away as they anonymously and generously serve others in need. They can be found in a kitchen, a backroom, or a park. If you look closely, you might even catch some of them handing out cheese sandwiches.

Chapter Eleven

Running with God – Mind, Body, and Spirit

AA's co-founder, Dr. Bob Smith, often spoke of the Bible, or the Good Book as he called it. He reminds 12-Steppers that in the Book of James it says, *"Faith without works is dead."* James 2:26 Action, and *more* action will be required. There is an African proverb which says, "When you pray, move your feet." I used to be a runner when I was in college and recently started running again after breaking my ankle and having surgery a few years ago. I've always loved running and I've found that incorporating exercise with my prayer life everyday has been extremely helpful on my recovery journey. I get some of my best direction while running with God. *"Let us run with endurance the race God has set before us."* Hebrews 12:1.

Interestingly, Bill Wilson, loved to walk and pray so

much that he almost included "prayer walking" into the steps. Perhaps wisely, he decided to keep the journey more general in nature. We all find God differently. While our search for God may look different, the fact remains that if we seek Him, we will *all* find Him. *"Ask, and it shall be given you; seek, and ye shall find; knock, and it shall be opened unto you." Matthew 7:7.*

I think one of the reasons I love running so much is because runners are often very positive people. Surely, the sport of running requires the athlete to have a certain mental tenacity which is strengthened by a positive, can-do mindset. Many of my running friends live out 1 Thessalonians 5:16-18 daily, *"Be joyful always; pray continually; give thanks in all circumstances, **for this is God's will for you in Christ Jesus."*** They are seeking God's will for their lives by being grateful, prayerful, and always joyful. My running friends inspire me daily.

Through the years, I've found that the same biblical principles needed to overcome my prescription addiction could be used to help me overcome any problem. To give you one example, after I broke my ankle and had subsequent surgery, I gained about 50 pounds. Sloth and gluttony seemed to be ruling my life during those long months. I was still a slave to sin, just another type of sin. So one day, after many, many 10th Steps and 11th Steps, I drew a triangle on a piece of paper. On the foundation of the triangle, I wrote, "God" and on one side I wrote, "Exercise" and on the other I wrote, "Food." My little diagram helps me remember Who holds the power to help me get better and what my game plan is to reach my goals. It looks similar to the AA symbol, which has "Recovery" as the foundation word and the sides of the triangle say "Unity" and "Service." I think of it this way: "Recovery" is the 12-Steps. They are the foundation of the process of getting better, but the sides, "Unity" and "Service" require me to get out of the house and get into action. Likewise, in my little health diagram, I surrendered everything to God. He is my foundation and the action to better health is my food plan and my exercise plan, which I have surrendered to Him. I have to do the work.

I love the triangle because it falls apart without all the sides being intact. The triangle itself is a "we" thing. I've tried just getting better on my own. I've tried just reading books and studying from home. But, it never works unless I get out there in service to others. Also, I've tried just relying on people and programs to help me recover from my addiction, losing weight, or surrendering to any other sin problem. It never worked without God as my foundation. I need *all* the sides of the triangle. It is the way that God designed our lives to work.

God has not only saved me from certain death from my prescription addiction, but He has helped me lose 60 pounds and get back in shape. Every Saturday morning, I meet some fun girlfriends at a recovery meeting and then we go for a run together. It is a precious time to talk with my friends about God, life, and recovery. We recently finished our first ½ marathon together and have signed up to run a marathon later this year. We decided to run the marathon as a relay team, however, because we've learned that this life is a "We" thing and we don't have to do it alone anymore.

I know today that all of the strongholds of sin in my life can be overcome with biblical application of 12-Step living. Sadly, the devil has strongholds over so many people, keeping them enslaved to every kind of addiction from food, spending, gambling, sexual addictions, smoking, and the list could go on ad infinitum. The good news is that basically anything can be conquered with God's help through the 12-Step process. We claim the promise of *Philippians 4:13, "I can do all things through Christ who strengthens me."* We serve a mighty and merciful God and He will help us if we seek Him.

On the way to church one morning, John and I were talking with the girls about how our **spiritual training** and **physical training** are so much alike. The first thing we came up with was the importance of **consistency** in our training both physical and spiritual. We have to suit up and show up on a daily basis if we are going to grow. We also agreed that to get stronger in our faith and in our bodies we must **increase the intensity** and go deeper in our training. Doing personal inventories, book studies, Bible studies as well as, boot camps, exercise classes and even running long distances helps us grow and get stronger.

We all agreed that training, both physical and spiritual, is *more fun with friends.* Impossible goals seem possible with friends we care about cheering us on and we can encourage them as well. John and I have traveled extensively with many recovery friends to conventions and conferences. Last year, we were at a convention in Hawaii with some recovery friends who love to workout. Everyday, we ran, hiked, did zumba, swam in the ocean, went to surfboard meetings, anything to move and have fun. One morning we did a hike up to Koko Head, which is a climb of about 1100 steps to the top of a beautiful mountain on Oahu. It was a tough climb. When we finally made it to the top, the view was breathtaking. We paused to express our gratitude for all that God was doing in our lives. I thought the hard part was behind me, but it turned out that the trip down the mountain was the really scary part. Each step was deliberate and purposeful.

One of the scariest parts was climbing over a bridge made of railroad ties which seem to hang in the air. The earth was a long way down and one misstep could mean disaster. Climbing up the mountain, I had been so focused on getting to the top that I didn't even think about the trip down. Many climbers stopped at that bridge and calculated the best approach to get down that section of the mountain. Some of them crawled on hands and knees, some seem to scoot on their backsides, but everyone was afraid. Terry, my husband's sponsor and our great friend, confidently said to our group, "It's just one step in front the other, just like we've been doing for the last several hundred steps." He stood up and began walking down. His wife, Dayna and I stood up and started taking one step at a time following Terry. After a few minutes of slow going, he reached for my hand and I reached for Dayna's hand. Together, we each took a step and then together, we took another step, and then another and another. Step by step we got over that bridge. We were amazed at how easy it became when we simply held hands and stepped together. Others around us followed our lead. I don't know why it was so much easier when we held hands and stepped together. We were still doing the action on our own, but suddenly a task which seemed overwhelming, if not impossible, was possible because we were doing it *together*. Physical training, spiritual training, and everything in life, is just plain easier and better with friends.

In recovery they say things like, "Stick with the winners and the winners are the people who are working the steps." Nobody does life perfectly, but stick with the friends who are trying to make things better rather than harder for others. Find the people who are in the solution and trying to follow God's will for their lives. Bill Wilson wrote about assessing the capacity for harm and the capacity for good in those who we would trust. I can tell you from personal experience that it's much easier to be that type of person for others when I'm surrounding myself with friends whose capacity for good is very great.

We have an old poem from the 1700's hanging in our home. It reminds us that each day our lives can be about making things better for the people around us, or our lives can be about making things harder for them.

Bag of Tools

by R.L Sharpe

Isn't it strange how princes and kings,
and clowns that caper in sawdust rings,
and common people, like you and me,
are builders for eternity?

Each is given a bag of tools;
a shapeless mass; a book of rules.
And each must make, ere life is flown,
A stumbling block, or a Stepping-Stone.

Everyday we get to choose how to use the "bag of tools" which God gave us. John and I are committed to building stepping stones for others with our God given "bag of tools." However, it's important to remember that the world is full of *both* kinds of builders. I don't want to be naïve about the fact that there are some who are stumbling block builders. Their capacity for harm is great. We have chosen to surround ourselves with hardworking stepping stone builders. They are so much more fun! Who will I surround myself with today? Who will I *be* for others today?

That morning, on the way to church, when we were

talking about how physical and spiritual training are so much alike, our oldest daughter Sarah, mentioned how we *need water* when we train our physical bodies and we need the Living Water of God for everything in life. Water, in every form is required in training. In my work as a Law Enforcement Chaplain, when we do death notifications, we are always giving people water. During a traumatic event it is easy to get dehydrated. Chaplain Frank Russell is always reminding us to make sure that we also give the victims we are serving, the **Living Water of God,** even if it's just covering the family in prayers. We know that even in the worst of life's tragedies, real hope can be found in God.

In physical training, I drink a great deal of water. I've started praying to drink in the power of God when I'm drinking water. At night, I go to sleep with a glass of water and when I drink it, I thank God for my day. In the morning, the first thing I do, even before coffee, is drink the rest of that water and ask God to guide me through the day ahead. *"My soul thirsts for God, for the living God."* Psalm 42:2. I pray that each day I will be lead by the Holy Spirit.

I'm reminded that I won't always feel inspired and sometimes I just have to trust the process. Several years ago, Pastor Henry Wells preached a sermon on surrender, specifically, he was talking about Romans 8:1-17 and "yielding to the Holy Spirit." He compared the power of a sailboat to the power of a rowboat. The rowboat, he explained, is powered by self-will. People physically row the boat where they want it to go, and usually, it's slow going in a rowboat. Contrarily, the sailboat is powered by the wind. He said that on a sailboat, there are so many things to do. Sailors work very hard, *especially* when there's no wind. They use their time preparing the boat. They know that their power comes from the wind, *not* from themselves. They have *faith* that the wind will come again. He asked a question. How often do you see a sailor pulling out the oars and rowing? Almost never. Yet, so often in life we get impatient, waiting on the wind, so we pull out the oars and start rowing our boat. Either we fear that the wind will never come again or that it will not come fast enough for us.

When the Wind is blowing and God is moving things around, I often visualize raising my white flag as a giant sail on a sailboat. By raising that flag I yield to the Holy Spirit as my source of power today. God resides deep down inside each one of us. We are powerless to live in God's will without yielding to the guidance of the Holy Spirit. God has already given us everything we need to live the life that He has planned for us. *"But they who wait for the LORD shall renew their strength; they shall mount up with wings like eagles; they shall run and not be weary; they shall walk and not faint."* Isaiah 40:31. All we have to do is raise our white flag, surrender to His will, keep readying our ship, and wait for the Wind, the **Living Water of God,** which will surely come again.

The last similarity in physical and spiritual training that we came up with on our drive to church that morning was when our youngest daughter, Katie, mentioned that *we grow through pain*. We talked about how pain brings blessings, but we cannot always see the blessings when we are in the pain. "The Big Book" reminds me that resentment is the number one offender and that even justified resentments are very dangerous for anyone seeking to live in God's will. Our family's biggest test of resentment came one day when our youngest daughter, Katie, was in kindergarten and attending an education enhancement program. I dropped her off and ran over to the gym to get in a quick workout. For some reason, when I got on that treadmill, I kept feeling pulled to leave the gym and go check on Katie. Normally, I would never stop a workout, once I'd started, but on that day, about 15 minutes in, I left the gym and drove back to the education center. When I got there, Katie was nowhere to be found. The director asked me to come into the office to fill out some paperwork. I just kept saying, "Where is Katie?" When he said she was in the bathroom, I rushed to the back of the building. To my horror, I could hear her screaming through the bathroom door, but I couldn't get in. The door was locked. I started yelling for someone to open the door! The director came running and used his key to open the bathroom door. Katie rushed into my arms and I could see that her mouth was bleeding. She'd clearly been hit in the face. Across the bathroom was a boy several years older than Katie with his pants down around his ankles. I immediately called 911 and then my husband.

The whole experience was truly horrific and surreal. The family of the other boy arrived and they were in another room crying. When John came *screeching up* in his truck, the police officer asked me if this was the father. When I said yes, he jumped in front of John, who looked like he was going to kill somebody. The police officer took Katie out of my arms and immediately handed her over to John. I watched the expression on my husband's face go from complete rage to sadness as he cried with our little girl.

We took Katie to the doctor that afternoon and thankfully, she had *not* been sexually assaulted. The officer at the scene said that had it been a few minutes later, who knows what could have happened. I was immediately grateful for the intuitive thought, I'd had on the treadmill that afternoon. I knew it was from God. I was grateful for His direction in my life that day. I knew from that moment that He had saved her from greater harm.

Katie's busted lip healed and our family literally loved her back to emotional health. There was, however, a change in Katie that day. Since that event, she's become a more cautious person than ever before. We didn't know it at the time, but Katie's kindergarten teacher was a 12-Stepping friend who loved her so much through that difficult time. She would call to check on her and loved on her for the entire school year. My husband kept saying that there was something really remarkable about this woman in Katie's life, but we couldn't put our finger on it. It wasn't until a few years later that we learned the truth about our similar journey. God had already chosen the perfect teacher to help Katie through that difficult year. Today, Sandy M. is my grand-sponsor and one of the most precious people in my life. I will never forget how she would lovingly assure me that God would make Katie stronger through this horrible experience.

Today, Katie is in high school and I'm pretty sure that her teacher was right. She is a gifted artist and plays the viola in the high school orchestra. We find it interesting that the viola is the instrument which provides the harmony to the violin and the entire orchestra. While her viola provides the harmony in the school's orchestra, her heart provides the harmony in our home.

Not only does Katie have a black belt in Taekwondo, but she's also an expert handgun marksman. Even with her keen awareness to danger, Katie is one of the kindest people I've ever known. She has compassion and empathy for others and seems to notice things that the rest of us don't even see. At school she is always reaching out to help children with special needs. She recognizes the lost or downtrodden in the room and constantly seeks them out to lift them up. At home, it is the same. Almost every time Katie peels an orange or cuts an apple or pear for herself, she cuts a second one to share with someone else. Over the years, I couldn't possibly count how many little bowls of fruit that child has brought me, and all of us in our family.

My husband will say, "With her constant thought of others, is it any wonder she is so joyful all the time?" She quite literally wakes up singing.

Katie responds to the needs of others in ways that most of us do not. Her intuitive thought is sometimes astonishing. Recently, I returned home from a Law Enforcement Chaplain call for a suicide of a high school student. We had spent the day talking to the family, fellow students, and teachers of a seventeen year old who took his own life. It had been a hard day of chaplain work, but Katie knew nothing about it. Still, on that afternoon, she made a picture for me. She is always creating things for us but this day she drew a cartoon of a discouraged fisherman laying down his fishing pole and walking away, while a giant fish was swimming right below his hook. Underneath the drawing it said, "Never give up." When I saw the picture, I sat down and cried. I didn't know that I needed to cry, but I did need to cry. In fact, I needed to sob. I needed to ask God, "Why did this child just give up?" And, "What happened to him?" Katie's picture helped "chaplain" the chaplain that day. Like so many other things she does, her actions helped healed my heart.

Katie has an unshakeable and steadfast faith in God and we've come to know for certain that, just as in the story of Joseph and his brothers from the Bible, what man meant for harm, God used for good. The harm that broken boy did to Katie, did not break her. In fact, she has allowed God to use that harm for good.

John and I didn't bounce back as quickly. We had weeks of sleepless nights. We were both *so* angry. I'm not even sure I can even explain how angry we actually were. I had never been that outraged by anything before. We talked to our sponsors, we prayed with each other and with friends, we talked to our pastor, we did inventories, we tried everything to let go of the rage we both felt. I decided to make sure this never happened to another child. In fact, I was going to shut down the whole nationwide organization. When executives from Chicago would call, I told them to talk to our lawyer. I was extremely mad and out to get even.

Over the next few months, several things happened. First, the education center was willing to make any changes necessary to keep children safe. Over time, I began to understand that they didn't really *intend* to hurt our child. This was a terrible accident. Yes, it could have been avoided, but it was still an accident. With the changes they were proposing to make across the country, this would not happen again to another child. Second, we learned more about this foreign-born boy and the abuse that he had suffered throughout his childhood. It did not mean that he shouldn't be held to account for his actions, or that he should be trusted around other young children ever again, but we were learning more about his tragic life.

Finally, the most important piece fell into place for us. It was a life-changing piece really. We began to see God's mercy in this horrific circumstance for Katie. God had given us mercy and had stopped this horrible act just in time. He had saved her and we knew that the last thing God would want us to do would be to start suing people and making this tragic situation even worse. When we understood the mercy that we had received, and I mean we understood it all the way deep down in our hearts, we could finally release this boy, his family, and the education center. With the changes they decided to make, we knew that we could show them mercy and simply walk away. In the end, we remembered that *"Mercy triumphs over judgment." James 2:13*

I know now that this story would never have ended as it did for our family without the prompting of the Holy Spirit, God's mercy, the spiritual guidance of faithful friends, family around us, and without the recovery tools we'd been so freely given. I don't know what would have happened to our family or to Katie without 12-Step recovery in our lives. I'm certain that all the energy we would have given to lawsuits and disputes would have hindered our ability to just love each other and heal. I know for sure that all of our lives would look very different today. Thankfully, we had so much love and support from people in our lives reminding us of passages like, *"Be merciful, just as your Father is merciful." Luke 6:36*

I've heard it said that grace is getting something that you don't deserve and mercy is not getting what you do deserve. If my Ruby Shoes each had a name, one would be called, "Grace" and the other named, "Mercy." I know that I've received an abundance of both. Grace keeps me grateful, and mercy changes lives. Mercy matters to the giver every bit as much as it matters to the receiver. Perhaps most importantly, mercy matters to God. I pray that He will help me spend the rest of my life being merciful to others, if for no other reason, than to demonstrate how grateful I am for all the grace and mercy I have received.

The Bible says *"What does the LORD require of you? To act justly and to love mercy and to walk humbly with your God." Micah 6:8.* Receiving mercy and being merciful to others are not the same thing. Through the 12-Steps, God has shown me how I've received *so* much mercy in my life, and I've come to know that I *must* be merciful to others. Sadly, we live in a world where everyone is trying to get ahead of each other, even if it means hurting someone else. These days, society seems to be teaching us to feel like victims, rather than victors in life. Subsequently, we show *less* mercy to those who've harmed us when they *need* mercy the very most.

Remember the image of Katie I saw when I lay dying in the hospital that October day? She was just a faint vision of a four-year-old child standing at the foot of my hospital bed. I've often wondered about seeing her. I may have even felt guilty that Katie was just standing at foot of my bed alone without her sister, Sarah. Why wasn't Sarah there? I love them *both* more than life itself. But, after this experience with

Katie, I wonder if perhaps our Omnipotent, all-knowing God, in His infinite wisdom, wanted me to remember that day *why* He needed me to come back to Him. You see Katie needed her mother and I needed to be whole for her in the coming months.

God knew that in the coming months, Katie would need a mother who was at Home with God, someone who could show her how to get back there herself. That precious image of Katie is a reminder for me of the promise I made to Him that day. It is my "Surrender Shift," something you will read about in the next chapter. As you will see, our "Surrender Shift" is a Holy and Sacred covenant with God. I believe that God wants me to fully understand and remember the promise I made to Him. Psalm 56:13 *"For You delivered me from death, even my feet from stumbling, to walk before God in the light of life."*

At the end of one of my running routes, there are three large rocks that are grouped together. There is a big rock with a smaller rock on each side. The group of rocks reminds me of those three crosses from long ago and the mercy that God gave the world from the cross of Jesus. Every time I run by those rocks I touch them and say, "Thank you, God" for all the mercy that I've received in my life. The man who hung on the cross with Jesus pleaded for mercy. Jesus answered him by saying, *"Truly I tell you, today you will be with me in paradise."* Luke 23:43. I, too, had pleaded for mercy. It was lying in a hospital bed, in my most sinful place, that I cried out for mercy. God said to me, "Come Home dear sinner, come Home."

I know today that I'm running with God. Everyday, come what may, I'm lacing up my Ruby Shoes and with both hands I'm holding onto God and my recovery friends. Together we are running towards Home.

Chapter Twelve

Surrender Shift

We used to have an apricot tree in our backyard. It produced the best apricots in the world. One night, after a big storm, the tree was blown over and we found it lying on the ground. My dad and John tried to stand it back up and build supports for the tree, but even still, it quickly began to die. We tried everything to save that tree, but John and Dad feared that the taproot of the tree had been severed. They told the girls and I that if the taproot is indeed severed, there is no saving the tree. They explained that a taproot is like the heart of the tree.

The taproot of recovery is found in our ability to yield to a higher power. I must fully accept that there is a God and I am *not* Him. It all begins with the complete surrender of Step One. I am powerless on my own. I would suggest that the taproot of the Gospel is the same. We are either fully relying on God or on self. Everyday, with every decision we make, we are either living in the flesh of this world or we are living in the Spirit. We cannot do both.

It was only after I decided to live in the Spirit rather than the flesh, that all of my questions changed. I used to say things like: "Why didn't I get everything I deserved in life?" And now I say, "Thank you God that I never got all that I deserved in life." I used to go places and say to myself, "Is this what I really need? Will this church, or this meeting, or this therapy group be able to give *me* what *I* need?" Now I try to remember to ask, "What can I *bring* to this group or gathering?" As Robin reminds me, even my prayers changed from, "God *help* me!" to, "God *use* me!" My whole attitude and outlook on life had changed.

As a Law Enforcement Chaplain, I am often blessed with the privilege of spending time with people who are in their last hours on earth. When a person knows they are in their last days of life, they usually make the shift from living in the flesh to living in the Spirit. It is what I call a Surrender Shift. It was when I lay dying in a hospital bed that the Surrender Shift happened for me and I continue to lean on this shift daily.

From what I've seen, a person's last words are usually real and authentic. I can tell you that the prayers I prayed to Jesus that October day were the most sincere petitions I could ever offer. Jesus' last words were sincere. At the last supper, the night before He died, Jesus summed everything up for His friends. He wanted to make *sure* that they remembered the main points or the taproot of His teachings: Seek God in everything you do and always love and serve one another.

Expressions of love and gratitude are common in a person's last hours of life. In all the years I've been doing this work, I've never been with a dying person who talked about vengeance, resentment, or settling some score. They never seem too concerned about their own personal situation and have little concern for material things of this world. They are, however, very concerned with the welfare of others and don't want to leave this world without expressing their love and gratitude for family and friends.

Finally, most dying people want to leave world with no regrets and many times they will finally lay down those rocks of sin and secrets they've been carrying around most of their lives. In alcoholism or addiction, the flesh is in control, but in recovery the Spirit is in control. When we finally make the Surrender Shift from living in the flesh to living in the Spirit, we truly make our home with, God. *"For everything in the world—the lust of the flesh, the lust of the eyes, and the pride of life—comes not from the Father but from the world. The world and its desires pass away, but whoever does the will of God lives forever."* 1 John 2:16-17

Perhaps the most beautiful lesson my 12-Stepping friends have taught me is that I don't have to be on my deathbed to abide with God. I have decided that I'm not going to wait until the very end to let go of my burdens and turn to God. I'm not going to wait to start really loving others. I'm going to do it right now.

The first part of the Serenity Prayer is said at most 12-Step recovery meetings. The entire prayer is one of the most beautiful surrender prayers in the world.

"God, grant me the Serenity to accept the things I cannot change, the courage to change the things I can, and the Wisdom to know the difference. Living one day at a time, enjoying one moment at a time; Accepting hardship as a pathway to peace; Taking as Jesus did, this sinful world as it is, not as I would have it; Trusting that You will make all things right if I surrender to Your will; So that I may be reasonably happy in this life and supremely happy with You forever in the next. Amen"

Surrendering my problems to God is not always an easy task. Sometimes I pray about something and turn it over to God, only to take it back again. One day a friend suggested that I get a "God Box." She suggested that when I am really ready to turn something over to God, I write it down on a piece of paper and place it in a box. Then, she said, offer another prayer of surrender and physically give that concern over to God. So, I started my little God Box many years ago and every time I struggle with a problem, I write it down, pray about it, and put it in my God Box. It helps me remember that I have *officially* given this to God.

One day, I took down my God Box and spread all of those prayer concerns out over my bed. Lying before me were prayers which stretched over 20 years of my life. I was overwhelmed with the all the answers that God had given me. They literally *covered* my bed. Over the years, bit-by-bit, God had answered *all* of those prayers for me. Some had been handled exactly as I had asked. Some had been answered differently, but it turns out, *so* much better than had it gone my way. My God Box has helped me to relax and trust in God. It has strengthened my faith in God and helped me understand His willingness to answer my prayers and take care of me. That little God Box has helped me remember and record all the things which God has done for me. *"I will recount the steadfast love of the LORD, the praises of the LORD, according to all that the LORD has granted us, and the great goodness to the house of Israel that he has granted them according to his compassion, according to the abundance of his steadfast love."* Isaiah 63:7 What started as a mustard seed of faith continues to grow every day. I know today that He loves me unconditionally and that He *always* has good things in store for me, even if I can't see them at the time.

My God Box helps me to consider what God has already done in my life and then trust Him with my future. I can *look back and thank God,* and then *look forward and trust God.*

Recovery, for me, was like looking at one of those trick pictures where there are two images to see inside one picture. It seemed like everyone around me could see both images right away. And as hard as I looked, I could often see just one picture. Then suddenly one day, I began to see the other image! I was so excited when I could finally see the image that everyone else had been seeing all along. And here's the beautiful part, once you've seen that other image, you can never _not_ see it again. Oh, I can walk away and not look at the picture at all, but every time I glance at it again, I can _see_ both images. My recovery journey has been exactly like seeing those two pictures inside of one. I'm not in control of when I will see the images; I just have to trust that eventually, if I keep trying, God will reveal them to me.

Just because we're getting better and living in God's will, doesn't mean that life won't be difficult at times. And as every football player knows, how he _practices_ the game everyday, will determine how he plays it the big games of his life. This is also true in our spiritual lives and our walk with God. As a Law Enforcement Chaplain, I see people every day who are thrust into perhaps the biggest game of their lives. With a sudden tragedy, everything in their world is changed forever. Some people are ready. They've made the Surrender Shift. They are living in the Spirit rather than the flesh. They have a strong faith in God and friends and family to lean on and help them through. But sadly, so many have no one to call and no faith to draw from. Any chaplain would tell you that those calls are the hardest. There are so many people in our world who are the lost, alone, and hopeless. But, it doesn't have to be this way.

My Texas family was thrust into the biggest game of their lives one day when a sudden and horrific tragedy happened to them. One horrible afternoon, my Uncle Mike was driving a tractor picking up hay bails to feed the cattle. In the course of moving the hay from the barn to the pasture, he accidentally backed over his two year old grandson. Luke was killed instantly. The grief everyone felt was beyond anything that any of us had ever experienced. In an instant, the whole world had changed.

I flew from California to Texas that next day and watched my family *demonstrate* God's love in *every* way possible. Their strong faith in God and their daily devotion to Him was obvious for everyone to see. How they loved and supported each other was a blessing to all. In the many years since that accident, I have never seen them get angry with each other over what happened. Never once have they acted like victims blaming each other for the accident. They never got into guilt or blame for what each other did, or didn't do, that tragic afternoon. My uncle and aunt and my cousin and her sweet husband, grieved and healed *together*, as a family, and with God's constant help. Rather than get into resentment, they loved each other and lifted each other up all the more.

There is a Chinese proverb that says, "Dig the well before you're thirsty." While no one is ever really prepared for this kind of tragedy, their well was ready when they were thirsty. They trusted God and sought the Living Water from the well they had already built.

Over the years, they've begun traveling to visit with other families who've had similar tragedies, always looking for a way to help others. Each one of them is stronger than before. You see, Luke's legacy for our family is one of *strengthening* our faith in God. In California and Texas, my family has always been a beautiful example of God's unending love. While my Texas family is not in 12-Step recovery, they all have a tremendous amount of faith in God. They understand the first step just as the Apostle Paul did when he talked about being powerless over our sinful natures. We *all* need God. It has been amazing to see how they practice the *same* principles and yet, have never actually taken the steps. Johnny Z reminds me that really we are all still working the same biblical principles. He jokingly says, "We 12-Steppers just have the *Cliff Notes.*" Following God's instructions, we all can make the Surrender Shift and then help others make the shift as well.

Some of my women's meetings have statues of elephants all around. Elephants are a great example of service in action. When an elephant gets sick, if it lies down, it dies. So, other elephants come and stand very close to the sick elephant, and quite literally, hold it up. By keeping the sick elephant on its feet, they keep it alive for another day.

"Elephants" in Lufkin, Texas ran to the Penn Farm that tragic afternoon when Luke died. They held up our family when we could not stand on our own. "Elephants" dressed as Law Enforcement Chaplains show up everyday across our country to help anonymous people face the most difficult days in their lifetimes. "Elephants" instinctively know that the first word in the First Step is "We." The Bible reminds us of this in Ecclesiastes 4:10 *"If one person falls, the other can reach out and help. But someone who falls alone is in real trouble."* Elephants, like faithful friends, never die alone.

It's easy to fill our time helping those who are fully surrendered and ready to get better. Unfortunately, we can't help everyone. Some people are like me in those early years. They are simply not ready to surrender and get better. The scripture in *Matthew 7:6 "Do not cast your pearls before swine"* is a caution about sharing ourselves with others. My mom is quick to remind me that that verse is not really about pigs at all. It is about remembering that you should only share your pearls with those who are ready to appreciate the value of what you are offering.

In being of service to others I need to remember that I can't help everyone. Sometimes I find myself trying everything to convince a friend to come into recovery and start taking the 12-Steps. I tell them about the power I had in the free gift of my Ruby Shoes. But, try as I might, they are just not ready. I find myself attempting to *sell* them on the idea of recovery. If only I could find the perfect way to explain it, maybe they would find their way home too.

A few years ago, my husband and I started really trying to help my sister-in-law, Lori, who was dying of alcoholism.

She had already lost custody of her children and she was living in Idaho drinking herself to death. John decided to go get her and put her into a recovery home close to where we live. The day he brought her home, I remember thinking she looked like she was nine months pregnant because her abdomen was so swollen due to liver damage. Her skin was yellow and ashen and her clothes were worn and dirty. She had thrown all of her belongings into a big black plastic bag and was ready to start over. We talked and prayed with her all the time. She was hopeful about a new life and a rebirth.

Over the next couple of years, Lori was in and out of recovery. She would leave a facility or get kicked out for drinking or taking prescription drugs and be on a run for several more months. Repeatedly, she would call John and ask him for help in getting sober again. John never refused to help Lori, although he knew that he could not *save* her. He was like my grandfather giving cheese sandwiches to the drunks in Lubbock, Texas long ago. He was just trying to love her the only way he knew how. John never judged Lori. He just helped her. He simply loved her right where she was. She had to find her own white flag and *she* had to wave it. Every time he would check her into another facility, we would pray that maybe this time it would work for her. However, recovery doesn't just happen for those who need it or even for those who really want it. Recovery works for those who DO it.

One morning at the office, John got a call from the

Sacramento Coroner's Office. They said that Lori had died from acute alcoholism. She had died alone in downtown Sacramento. For a whole month, no one even knew where she was. We were devastated by the loss of Lori. We knew that this did not have to happen. But, we found comfort in the knowledge that we serve a mighty and merciful God who loves her more than we could ever know.

Lori never picked up the pearls which we tried so desperately to give her. For so many years, I never picked up the pearls so many others were trying to give me. Lori and I were both in a place where we could not appreciate the value of those precious pearls. We just trampled on the pearls. Surrender never came for Lori and almost came too late for me.

We grieve the loss of Lori still today. We will grieve her forever. But, every time we work with another alcoholic, we are grateful for the chance to do so. Healing in our lives comes as we continue to give our pearls away to another hopeless friend.

My prayer is that Lori, too, was found by her Heavenly Father in those quiet moments with her Creator before she died. I pray that Lori made a peaceful Surrender Shift from living in the world of the flesh to the world of the Spirit. *"For the Son of Man came to seek and to save the lost." Luke 19:10*

Michele Zumwalt

Chapter Thirteen

Home

When Dorothy and I arrived safely back home, everything had changed forever. Anyone watching the movie, "The Wizard of Oz" knew it was true. Something profound had changed in Dorothy. She had a new attitude and outlook on life. Before the tornado, she ran around complaining, frustrated that no one would listen to her. After the tornado that almost killed her and being lost in a strange land for sometime, she returned home a different person. From then on Dorothy had a heart full of love and gratitude for all that she had on that little farm in Kansas. She was different. In the blink of an eye, with the click of a heel, she had changed.

Waving my white flag, from a hospital bed, I returned home. Like Dorothy's homecoming, everything had changed forever in me. Everyone knew it. My husband and family knew from the moment they saw me in the ICU, I was different. I had changed. But, here's the main point: *I didn't do it. God did.* He gave me the gift of Jesus. *"He brought me up also out of a horrible pit, out of the miry clay, and set my feet upon a rock." Psalm 40:2.* All I had to do was say, "Yes, Lord!" My prayers were answered and God had changed me.

Sometimes I wonder how I got to this place. How did I go from being a completely lost and broken person to where I am today? How did I go from jail to Law Enforcement Chaplain, from prescription addict to teaching doctors about prescription addiction, from lost to found, from addiction to recovery, and from dying to truly living? It came through daily application of 12-Step, biblical living. Remember, a bird with a broken wing, once healed, can often fly higher than ever before. Here's the really good part; *if I can get better, anyone can.*

Before I do public speaking events, I always say a prayer for the people I will be addressing. I know that God already knows the audience and every need of every person in attendance. I pray that He will direct my words and use me for His good purposes. I ask for guidance on the main point or the taproot of my talk. His answer is always the same: Tell them to stop trying to *earn* My love because they already have it. Tell them how much I love them. Tell them that you were a dying person and, in your most sinful place, I *still* loved you and I saved you.

If you don't hear anything else from my story, I pray

that you will hear me say that God loves you completely right where you are. Right here and right now, you are enough. You do not have to earn His love. You have it. You simply need to surrender and come Home to Him.

The Bible talks about the streets of gold in our Heavenly Home. In sharp contrast, the metaphorical yellow brick road, with the poppy fields on either side, led nowhere. Nothing can mimic the glory of God. But, as I travel down the 12-Step path I'm on today, I know I'm seeing glimpses of my Heavenly Home and the grandeur of the beautiful streets paved with gold. By following His instructions, I know that today, no matter what happens in life, I can be at Home with God. We all can. *"Jesus replied, "Anyone who loves me will obey my teaching. My Father will love them, and we will come to them and make our home with them." John 14:23*

Years ago, when I was in my very first detox facility, my mother gave me a magnet which still hangs on my refrigerator today. On it are the words: *"For I know the plans I have for you, says the Lord...to give you a future and a hope."* Jeremiah 29:11. I kept that magnet all these years because it reminds me of how foreign those words were for me then. I was so lost, I couldn't imagine a God who had plans, a future, and hope for me. Today, my life is full of hope and my future is secure in Him. *"Fear not, for I am with you; be not dismayed, for I am your God; I will strengthen you, I will help you, I will uphold you with my righteous right hand." Isaiah 41:10*

One night, when I spoke at a meeting, I mentioned

the magnet that Mom had given me and it's promise of hope. When the meeting was over, a lady came up to me and said she had that exact quote (as she called it) tattooed on her ankle. She wanted to know the source of the quote. I told her it was from the Bible, Jeremiah 29:11. She looked stunned for a moment and then she started to cry. I told her I was amazed by her tattoo and how far God had gone to *seek* her out. Together, we both cried tears of joy.

I was inspired to write my story while I was running and praying one day. I picked up a piece of paper on the trail in front of me which said: "Go Home and Tell Your Story." I knew that God was speaking directly to me. He said in *Mark 5:19 "Go home to your friends and tell them the great things which the Lord has done for you..."* It has taken me a long time to get back Home, but God knew that I could only tell this story *while being at HOME with Him.*

It is my sincerest prayer that my story provides some hope for those who are lost and cannot find their way back home. We don't ever have to be lost again! We don't have to go looking for chemical solutions to our spiritual problems anymore. We don't have to spend our lives sleeping in poppy fields or drifting off over the rainbow. We don't have to earn God's love or ticket home by capturing the world's stupid brooms. You see, we already have the power of God and His LOVE that dwells within us. We've had it all along.

My closing prayer for you is this, *"May the God of hope fill you with all joy and peace in believing, so that by the power of* the Holy Spirit you may abound in hope." Romans 15:13 and "May Christ through your faith dwell in your hearts. May you be rooted deep in love and founded securely on love," Ephesians 3:17 and may you always feel and know that "my cup runneth over. Surely goodness and mercy shall follow me all the days of my life, and I will dwell in the house of the LORD forever." Psalm 23:5-6.

And that my friend, is Home.

ABOUT THE AUTHOR

After a near death experience from an addiction to prescription drugs, Michele Zumwalt has dedicated her life to helping others find hope and recovery. She has a steadfast faith in God and her life's purpose is found in serving Him by serving others. Michele has been the keynote speaker and teacher for recovery and medical groups, such as, the University of California, Davis, Medical Students and many others. Michele is an advocate for public policy change and has been awarded a signed copy of *her law* by the California Legislature. She is a Law Enforcement Chaplain in the County of Sacramento where she assists with death notifications, speaks at police briefings, and is a Critical Incident Stress Debrief Facilitator assisting Police Officers after Officer Involved Shootings. Michele has a Bachelor of Science Degree in Business Administration, Marketing. She serves as a Finance Elder for Fair Oaks Presbyterian Church. Michele is on the Board of Directors for the American River Alano which serves thousands seeking 12-Step recovery meetings every week in the Sacramento area. She's the Executive Director of a non-profit children's charity, Contractors Caring for Kids, which she and her husband, John, founded in 1995 and has raised over 500,000.00 for local children in need. She is a devoted wife and mother of two beautiful daughters. Finally, she is a runner...

"Let us run with endurance the race that is set before us, looking to Jesus, the founder and perfecter of our faith." Hebrews 12:1-2

Mile 12 at the Shamrock Half Marathon.

Prayers from this book:

Third Step Prayer:

"God, I offer myself to Thee--to build with me and to do with me as Thou wilt. Relieve me of the bondage of self, that I may better do Thy will. Take away my difficulties, that victory over them may bear witness to those I would help of Thy Power, Thy Love, and Thy Way of life. May I do Thy will always! Amen."

Seventh Step Prayer:

"My Creator, I am now willing that you would have all of me, good and bad. I pray that You remove from me every single defect of character which stands in the way of my usefulness to You and my fellows. Grant me strength as I go from here to do Your bidding. Amen."

Serenity Prayer:

"God, grant me the Serenity to accept the things I cannot change, the courage to change the things I can, and the Wisdom to know the difference. Living one day at a time, enjoying one moment at a time; Accepting hardship as a pathway to peace; Taking as Jesus did, this sinful world as it is, not as I would have it; Trusting that You will make all things right if I surrender to Your will; So that I may be reasonably happy in this life and supremely happy with You forever in the next. Amen"

Eleventh Step Prayer:

The Prayer of St. Francis of Assisi
Lord, make me a channel of thy peace,
that where there is hatred, I may bring love,
that where there is wrong, I may bring the spirit of forgiveness,
that where there is discord, I may bring harmony,
that where there is error, I may bring truth,
that where there is doubt, I may bring faith,
that where there is despair, I may bring hope,
that where there are shadows, I may bring light,
that where there is sadness, I may bring joy.
Lord, grant that I may seek rather to comfort than to be comforted,
to understand, than to be understood,
to love, than to be loved.
For it is by self-forgetting that one finds. It is by forgiving that one
is forgiven. It is by dying that one awakens to eternal life. Amen.

The Lord's Prayer:

Our Father, which art in heaven,
Hallowed be thy Name.
Thy Kingdom come.
Thy will be done in earth,
As it is in heaven.
Give us this day our daily bread.
And forgive us our trespasses,
As we forgive them that trespass against us.
And lead us not into temptation,
But deliver us from evil.
For thine is the kingdom,
The power, and the glory,
For ever and ever. Amen.

Made in the USA
Charleston, SC
15 November 2015